Modern Critical Interpretations

F. Scott Fitzgerald's
The Great Gatsby

CHELSEA HOUSE PUBLICATIONS
Modern Critical Interpretations

The Oresteia
Beowulf
The General Prologue to
  The Canterbury Tales
The Pardoner's Tale
The Knight's Tale
The Divine Comedy
Exodus
Genesis
The Gospels
The Iliad
The Book of Job
Volpone
Doctor Faustus
The Revelation of St.
  John the Divine
The Song of Songs
Oedipus Rex
The Aeneid
The Duchess of Malfi
Antony and Cleopatra
As You Like It
Coriolanus
Hamlet
Henry IV, Part I
Henry IV, Part II
Henry V
Julius Caesar
King Lear
Macbeth
Measure for Measure
The Merchant of Venice
A Midsummer Night's
  Dream
Much Ado About
  Nothing
Othello
Richard II
Richard III
The Sonnets
Taming of the Shrew
The Tempest
Twelfth Night
The Winter's Tale
Emma
Mansfield Park
Pride and Prejudice
The Life of Samuel
  Johnson
Moll Flanders
Robinson Crusoe
Tom Jones
The Beggar's Opera
Elegy
Paradise Lost
The Rape of the Lock
Tristram Shandy
Gulliver's Travels

Evelina
The Marriage of Heaven
  and Hell
Songs of Innocence and
  Experience
Jane Eyre
Wuthering Heights
Don Juan
The Rime of the Ancient
  Mariner
Bleak House
David Copperfield
Hard Times
A Tale of Two Cities
Middlemarch
The Mill on the Floss
Jude the Obscure
The Mayor of
  Casterbridge
The Return of the Native
Tess of the D'Urbervilles
The Ode of Keats
Frankenstein
Vanity Fair
Barchester Towers
The Prelude
The Red Badge of
  Courage
The Scarlet Letter
The Ambassadors
Daisy Miller, The Turn
  of the Screw, and
  Other Tales
The Portrait of a Lady
Billy Budd, Benito Cer-
  eno, Bartleby the Scriv-
  ener, and Other Tales
Moby Dick
The Tales of Poe
Walden
The Adventures of
  Huckleberry Finn
The Life of Frederick
  Douglass
Heart of Darkness
Lord Jim
Nostromo
A Passage to India
Dubliners
A Portrait of the Artist as
  a Young Man
Ulysses
Kim
The Rainbow
Sons and Lovers
Women in Love
1984
Major Barbara

Man and Superman
Pygmalion
St. Joan
The Playboy of the
  Western World
The Importance of Being
  Earnest
Mrs. Dalloway
To the Lighthouse
My Antonia
An American Tragedy
Murder in the Cathedral
The Waste Land
Absalom, Absalom!
Light in August
Sanctuary
The Sound and the Fury
The Great Gatsby
A Farewell to Arms
The Sun Also Rises
Arrowsmith
Lolita
The Iceman Cometh
Long Day's Journey Into
  Night
The Grapes of Wrath
Miss Lonelyhearts
The Glass Menagerie
A Streetcar Named
  Desire
Their Eyes Were
  Watching God
Native Son
Waiting for Godot
Herzog
All My Sons
Death of a Salesman
Gravity's Rainbow
All the King's Men
The Left Hand of
  Darkness
The Brothers Karamazov
Crime and Punishment
Madame Bovary
The Interpretation of
  Dreams
The Castle
The Metamorphosis
The Trial
Man's Fate
The Magic Mountain
Montaigne's Essays
Remembrance of Things
  Past
The Red and the Black
Anna Karenina
War and Peace

These and other titles in preparation

Modern Critical Interpretations

F. Scott Fitzgerald's
The Great Gatsby

Edited and with an introduction by
Harold Bloom
Sterling Professor of the Humanities
Yale University

Chelsea House Publishers •
New York/New Haven/Philadelphia

Austin Community College
Learning Resources Center

ᵢₐ

Copyright © 1986 by Chelsea House Publishers, a division
of Chelsea House Educational Communications, Inc.

3   5   7   9   8   6   4

Introduction copyright © 1986 by Harold Bloom

All rights reserved. No part of this publication may be
reproduced or transmitted, in any form or by any means,
without the written permission of the publisher.

Printed and bound in the United States of America

Library of Congress Cataloging in Publication Data
Main entry under title:
F. Scott Fitzgerald's The great gatsby.

(Modern critical interpretations)
Bibliography: p.
Includes index.
    1. Fitzgerald, F. Scott (Francis Scott), 1896–1940. Great
Gatsby—Addresses, essays, lectures.   I. Bloom, Harold.
II. Series.
PS3511.I9G837   1986   813'.52   85-17500
ISBN 0-87754-901-X

Contents

Editor's Note   vii
Introduction   1
    Harold Bloom

The Structure of *The Great Gatsby*   5
    Kenneth Eble

Scott Fitzgerald's Criticism of America   11
    Marius Bewley

Two Versions of the Hero   29
    David Parker

Gatsby and the Failure of the Omniscient "I"   45
    Ron Neuhaus

Another Reading of *The Great Gatsby*   57
    Keath Fraser

Oral Aggression and Splitting   71
    A. B. Paulson

The Great Gatsby   87
    Brian Way

The *Waste Land* Myth and Symbols in *The Great Gatsby*   109
    Letha Audhuy

Chronology   123

Contributors   125

Bibliography   127

Acknowledgments   129

Index   131

Editor's Note

This volume represents a selection of the best criticism available on F. Scott Fitzgerald's now classic short novel, *The Great Gatsby*. It begins with the editor's introduction, which centers upon the book's relation to the poetry of John Keats, and so in a sense to Fitzgerald's own "negative capability."

The eight essays and extracts gathered together here follow in the chronological sequence of their publication, starting with Kenneth Eble's consideration of the novel's structure in the light of the revisions it underwent in manuscript.

Marius Bewley's remarkable reading follows, with its unrivaled balance between the complex senses in which *The Great Gatsby* is at once Fitzgerald's criticism of, and tribute to, the American dream. In David Parker's shrewd "Two Visions of the Hero," the novel is juxtaposed to Browning's great monologue "Childe Roland to the Dark Tower Came," as two versions of a romance tradition older than America.

With the essay by Ron Neuhaus, we move to a different juxtaposition of Fitzgerald and his tradition, particularly as exemplified by the influence of Conrad upon *The Great Gatsby*. Neuhaus ingeniously suggests that the weakness of Carraway, Fitzgerald's omniscient "I," compared to Conrad's Marlow, becomes an intriguing element of aesthetic survival for the novel, since it helps us to reject all moralizing that might damage *The Great Gatsby*'s fragile Romanticism. This contrasts to Keath Fraser's reading, where Carraway's narrative opacities are subtly read as signs of an ambiguous sexuality that pervades the novel.

This ambiguity is explored more categorically in A. B. Paulson's overtly psychoanalytic study of the novel as a complex instance of the defensive stances that Freud called "oral aggression" and "splitting." In Paulson's reading, the ambiguity's focus moves from Carraway to Jordan Baker and to Daisy. With Brian Way's study, we move to the very different orientation of a social vision, which illuminates the novel by way of comparisons with *Madame Bovary*, and with Shakespeare's Falstaff.

The final essay, by the French critic Letha Audhuy, complements Parker's earlier reading by analyzing the direct influence of Eliot's *The Waste Land* upon *The Great Gatsby*. Since, in the editor's judgment, Eliot's poem was massively indebted to Victorian waste land visions, including Browning's "Childe Roland" and Percivale's quest for "The Holy Grail" *(Idylls of the King)* there is an intensification of the entire allusive structure of *The Great Gatsby* when Fitzgerald's finest achievement is contextualized in its romance tradition.

Introduction

Lionel Trilling justly observed of *The Great Gatsby* that "if the book grows in weight of significance with the years, we can be sure that this could not have happened had its form and style not been as right as they are." Trilling, critically accurate, was also prophetic in regard to the novel's augmenting importance. Indeed, that importance transcends *The Great Gatsby*'s formal achievement, its aesthetic dignity of shape and style. The book has become part of what must be called the American mythology, just as Fitzgerald himself now possesses mythological status, like Hemingway, or, in a different sense, Norman Mailer. Myth is gossip grown old, according to the modern Polish aphorist, Stanislaw Lec. Fitzgerald's social aspirations, his mode of living, his marriage to Zelda, his "crack-up" and death at the age of forty-four: these now have aged into myth. But that is popular myth; *The Great Gatsby* is myth of another mode also, the mode of John Keats, whose spirit never departs from Fitzgerald's best writing.

The Great Gatsby is a lyrical novel, a triumph of sensibility, worthy of the poet who wrote *Lamia*, *The Fall of Hyperion*, the great Odes, and "La Belle Dame Sans Merci." Consider a single scene in *Gatsby*, towards the end of chapter 5. Gatsby is showing Daisy (and Nick Carraway, the Conradian narrator) his house. They enter his bedroom, where Daisy takes up a hairbrush of "pure dull gold" and smooths her hair, causing Gatsby, too happy in her happiness, to laugh too boisterously:

> "It's the funniest thing, old sport," he said hilariously. "I can't—When I try to—"
> He had passed visibly through two states and was entering upon a third. After his embarrassment and his unreasoning joy he was consumed with wonder at her presence. He had been full of the idea so long, dreamed it right through to the end, waited with his teeth set, so to speak, at the inconceivable pitch of intensity. Now, in the reaction, he was running down like an overwound clock.
> Recovering himself in a minute he opened for us two hulking patent cabinets which held his massed suits and dressing-gowns and ties, and his shirts, piled like bricks in stacks a dozen high.
> "I've got a man in England who buys me clothes. He sends over a selection of things at the beginning of each season, spring and fall."
> He took out a pile of shirts and began throwing them, one by one, before us, shirts of sheer linen and thick silk and fine flannel, which lost their folds as they fell and covered the table in many-colored disarray. While we admired he brought more and the soft rich heap mounted higher—shirts with stripes and scrolls and plaids in coral and apple-green and lavender and faint orange, with monograms of Indian blue. Suddenly with a strained sound, Daisy bent her head into the shirts and began to cry stormily.
> "They're such beautiful shirts," she sobbed, her voice muffled in the thick folds. "It makes me sad because I've never seen such—such beautiful shirts before."

This grand passage is an epitome of the novel, and an apotheosis of Fitzgerald's Keatsian art. Gatsby, piling up the soft rich heap in its many-colored disarray of "stripes and scrolls and plaids in coral and apple-green and lavender and faint orange, with monograms of Indian blue," is surely a version of another passionate lover: Porphyro in *The Eve of St. Agnes*:

> Then by the bed-side, where the faded moon
> Made a dim, silver twilight, soft he set
> A table, and, half anguished, threw thereon
> A cloth of woven crimson, gold, and jet:—
> O for some drowsy Morphean amulet!
> The boisterous, midnight, festive clarion,
> The kettle-drum, and far-heard clarinet,
> Affray his ears, though but in dying tone:—
> The hall door shuts again, and all the noise is gone.
>
> And still she slept an azure-lidded sleep,
> In blanchèd linen, smooth, and lavendered,
> While he from forth the closet brought a heap
> Of candied apple, quince, and plum, and gourd;
> With jellies soother than the creamy curd,
> And lucent syrups, tinct with cinnamon;
> Manna and dates, in argosy transferred
> From Fez; and spiced dainties, every one,
> From silken Samarcand to cedared Lebanon.
>
> These delicates he heaped with glowing hand
> On golden dishes and in baskets bright
> Of wreathed silver: sumptuous they stand
> In the retired quiet of the night,
> Filling the chilly room with perfume light.—
> 'And now, my love, my seraph fair, awake!
> Thou art my heaven, and I thine eremite:
> Open thine eyes, for meek St. Agnes' sake,
> Or I shall drowse beside thee, so my soul doth ache.'

The heap of edible dainties and delicates has been replaced by the soft rich heap of multi-colored shirts, and Madeline is asleep while Daisy is awake, yet Fitzgerald's exquisitely displaced allusion is clear enough. The masterful revision that makes Fitzgerald's scene into high art is Daisy's sudden storm of tears as she so erotically bends her head into the shirts. A further revision is even more in the Keatsian spirit, when it becomes clear to Gatsby how doom-eager and idealized his passion truly has become, profoundly in excess of the object:

After the house, we were to see the grounds and the swimming pool, and the hydroplane and the mid-summer flowers—but outside Gatsby's window it began to rain again, so we stood in a row looking at the corrugated surface of the Sound.

"If it wasn't for the mist we could see your home across the bay," said Gatsby. "You always have a green light that burns all night at the end of your dock."

Daisy put her arm through his abruptly, but he seemed absorbed in what he had just said. Possibly it had occurred to him that the colossal significance of that light had now vanished forever. Compared to the great distance that had separated him from Daisy it had seemed very near to her, almost touching her. It had seemed as close as a star to the moon. Now it was again a green light on a dock. His count of enchanted objects had diminished by one.

Working as Keats told Shelley a poet must work—"*an artist* must serve Mammon—. . . and 'load every rift' of your subject with ore"—Fitzgerald too follows a Spenserian loading of every rift, and ends his novel with a return of that green light of the ideal:

And as I sat there brooding on the old, unknown world, I thought of Gatsby's wonder when he first picked out the green light at the end of Daisy's dock. He had come a long way to this blue lawn, and his dream must have seemed so close that he could hardly fail to grasp it. He did not know that it was already behind him, somewhere back in that vast obscurity beyond the city, where the dark fields of the republic rolled on under the night.

Gatsby believed in the green light, the orgiastic future that year by year recedes before us. It eluded us then, but that's no matter—tomorrow we will run faster, stretch out our arms farther. . . . And one fine morning—

So we beat on, boats against the current, borne back ceaselessly into the past.

In so concluding, Fitzgerald consciously culminated a Keatsian version of the quest. The man of imagination, however compromised, quests perpetually for an immortal female, more daemonic than human. Poor Daisy may seem an inadequate version of a Lamia, but she is precisely a possible American Belle Dame Sans Merci of 1925, and Gatsby is her inevitable victim, who does not want to know better, and so is not deceived. His marvellous dismissal of Daisy's love for her dreadful husband—"In any case, it was just personal"—is his clear self-recognition. It cannot matter that Daisy is an absurd object, because Gatsby's drive is Transcendental. What matters is what the Yeatsian quester of *A Full Moon in March* calls "the image in my head." In love with that image, Gatsby truly is self-engendered, and dies more than adequately.

If there is an American Sublime, going beyond irony, in modern American fiction, then it is located most centrally in *The Great Gatsby*.

Fitzgerald fittingly could have chosen for an epigraph to his novel the final stanza of the "Ode on Melancholy" by Keats:

> She dwells with Beauty—Beauty that must die;
>   And Joy, whose hand is ever at his lips
> Bidding adieu; and aching Pleasure nigh,
>   Turning to poison while the bee-mouth sips:
> Ay, in the very temple of Delight
>   Veiled Melancholy has her sovereign shrine,
>   Though seen of none save him whose strenuous tongue
> Can burst Joy's grape against his palate fine;
>   His soul shall taste the sadness of her might,
>   And be among her cloudy trophies hung.

Gatsby, whatever his limitations, had been that quester, and is always to be remembered as one of those trophies, and not the least among them.

The Structure of
The Great Gatsby

Kenneth Eble

The Great Gatsby suffers as much as most good novels from having its plot thus extracted and set forth. Directness and simplicity are fundamental characteristics of the novel, but the technique of slowly and enigmatically creating the character of Gatsby, of seeing the novel largely through Carraway's eyes, and of making the most of atmosphere and suggestion make the novel seem longer than its actual length of about fifty thousand words. The story takes place within a single summer, but the chronology does not move straightforwardly along. The first fifty-six pages relate the events of three nights several weeks apart in which Nick Carraway appears at East Egg with his cousin Daisy and Jordan Baker; in New York with Tom Buchanan and Myrtle Wilson; and in West Egg with Jay Gatsby. Immediately after these scenes, Carraway breaks into the narrative to give an account of his ordinary life during and after the events described. The introductory section comes to a kind of climax when Carraway's interest in Jordan Baker leads to two crucial observations: Jordan is "incurably dishonest," and he himself is "one of the few honest people I have ever known."

The next section begins with the Gatsby of parties and rumors. The date, appropriately noted on an old timetable, is July, 1922. The people who come to Gatsby's house are presented in mock-epic fashion. It is the catalogue of ships; the summoning of forces. It even ends with an epic cadence: "All these people came to Gatsby's house in the summer." Carraway, who meets Gatsby, hears from him a history as fantastic in its entirety as the single bit of documentary evidence he offers as proof. The scene at Gatsby's party is parallel with the next scene, a meeting

From *F. Scott Fitzgerald.* Copyright © 1977 by G. K. Hall & Co.

between Nick, Gatsby, and Meyer Wolfsheim, the man who fixed the 1919 World Series. At this point, the narrative shifts to Jordan Baker and, through a story she tells to Nick Carraway, back in time to Daisy Fay's house in Louisville in 1917. This was where Jay Gatsby, an obscure second lieutenant, met and fell in love with Daisy. By the end of chapter 5, then, the reader is able to see the Gatsby of the past and of the present; he still remains something of a mystery, but the forces drawing the various characters together are clearly evident at this point.

Chapter 5, the meeting between Gatsby and Daisy, is at the precise center of the book. The scene is the most static in the novel. It is, by design, timeless. For a moment, after the confusion of the meeting, the rain, and his own doubts, Gatsby holds past and present together. As if to prolong this scene in the reader's mind, chapter 6 leaves the narrative, shifts the scene to the reporter inquiring about Gatsby, and fills in Gatsby's real past. "I take advantage of this short halt," Nick Carraway says, "while Gatsby, so to speak, caught his breath." The deliberate pause illustrates the care with which the novel is constructed. The Gatsby of his self-created present is contrasted with the Gatsby of his real past, and the moment is prolonged before the narrative moves on. The rest of chapter 6 focuses on the first moment of disillusion—Gatsby's peculiar establishment as seen through Daisy's eyes. It ends with Gatsby's central speech: " 'Can't repeat the past?' he cried incredulously. 'Why of course you can!' "

With the beginning of chapter 7, the novel gains momentum and the mood changes. The lights in Gatsby's house fail to go on. Heat and sweat become the dominant images. It is as if Fitzgerald were moving the reader from Father Schwartz's early remark in "Absolution" that "When a lot of people get together in the best places things go glimmering," to his later warning: "But don't get up close, because if you do you'll only feel the heat and the sweat and the life." All the climactic events are packed into this chapter, the longest in the book—almost twice as long as any of the others. The prose quickens; events move from the trip to New York and Gatsby's first clash with Tom Buchanan to the accidental death of Myrtle Wilson and the vigil Gatsby keeps outside Daisy's window.

The sustained narrative obviously cannot be pushed much further without a break, and the chapter ends with Gatsby "standing there in the moonlight—watching over nothing." The first part of chapter 8 pauses while Gatsby and Nick await the events to come. This was the night, Carraway says, that Gatsby told him the story (its factual details have been told earlier in the novel) of his early life. The purpose of the telling here is not to reveal facts but to try to understand the character of Gatsby's passion. The final understanding is reserved for one of those precisely right utterances by which the characters reveal themselves so often in this novel: "In any case," Gatsby says, speaking of Daisy's love for Tom, "it was just personal." The scene ends with Nick pronouncing a kind of benediction over Gatsby as he leaves, "They're a rotten crowd. You're worth the whole damn bunch put together." The resolution comes quickly. The narrator makes a shift in scene, a slight flashback in time, and, as if reported by a detached but on-the-spot observer, Wilson is followed step by step until he finds Gatsby floating on a rubber mattress in his pool and kills him and then himself.

The forward movement of the novel stops there. Chapter 9 is told as it lives in Nick Carraway's memory two years later. The last tales of Gatsby come through Wolfsheim and Mr. Gatz. Like "Benjamin Button," Gatsby's story is a tale of growth to birth. We arrive inexorably in the past—September 12, 1906, to be exact—and read the copy-book maxims of the young James Gatz. The last section pushes Nick Carraway similarly back in time, with that memorable passage about his memories of coming back West from preparatory school. The last page pushes Gatsby, Nick, Daisy—all of us—back into the past. The Dutch sailors' eyes are our eyes, and we are indeed—in the very movement of the novel—"boats against the current, borne back ceaselessly into the past."

This detailed examination of the structure of *The Great Gatsby* calls attention to one of the novel's great virtues: the tight inevitability of its construction. Abstracting from specific details, we see a pattern of movement and withdrawal, and at the center, a moment of dead calm, possession. The scenic character of the first half is heightened by the swiftness of the narrative in the last half. And much of the novel's success in creating a feeling of timelessness despite the story's sharply contemporary events is traceable to the effect of matching the swiftly on-going narrative with a less swift but powerful movement into the past. The image of "the old island that flowered once for Dutch sailors' eyes" has been expertly prepared for, and the story comes to its final line with the inevitability of all high art.

The construction of *The Great Gatsby* is the more remarkable because the crucial ordering of the material did not come until after the book was in galley proof. In its simplest form, the change was that of taking the true story of James Gatz's past out of chapter 8 and bringing it forward to the beginning of chapter 6. Thus, as I have noted, the static center of the novel—that moment when Gatsby is alone with Daisy and can hold past and present together—extends itself on into chapter 7. The story of the Gatsby who sprang from his Platonic conception of himself is placed precisely where it will make its greatest impact: between that moment of suspended time at the end of chapter 5 and Gatsby's beginning to be aware of the vanity of his own dreams in the party scene of chapter 6.

That Fitzgerald was consciously striving for this effect is indicated not merely by the transposition of this section but by the very careful and extensive revisions made on almost every page of the galley proofs of these central chapters. The second party, for example, has been changed in many subtle and moving ways. That remarkable image of the motion picture director and his star was originally a part of Gatsby's first party. Fitzgerald apparently recognized its power of "magic suggestiveness" when he removed it there and wrote it into the later scene:

> It was like that. Almost the last thing I remember was standing with Daisy and watching the moving-picture director and his Star. They were still under the white-plum tree and their faces were touching except for a pale, thin ray of moonlight between. It occurred to me that he had been very slowly bending toward her all evening to attain this proximity, and even while I watched I saw him stoop one ultimate degree and kiss at her cheek.

Such a passage is one of dozens which could be cited to illustrate the excellence of Fitzgerald's style, maintained at its highest degree of polish in *The Great Gatsby*. The big changes in the galley proofs are the transposing of materials and the rewriting of scenes involved in that transposition. But throughout the galleys, small changes continually occur to remind us of how Fitzgerald's highly polished style was achieved.

Many of these changes are in individual words: "silhouette" for "shadow," "vanished" for "gone," "soiled" for "spotted," "the blue honey" of the Mediterranean for "fairy blue." A few change the inflections of a speaker's voice: "snapped" instead of "said," cried "ecstatically" instead of "excitedly," "looked at me absently" instead of "replied." Occasionally a better phrase is found: "freedom from money" rather than "spending capacity"; "corky but rather impressive claret" for "wine"; "as if his sturdy physical egotism no longer nourished his peremptory heart" for "as if his sturdy physical egotism wasn't enough for him anymore." A slight change, like having Myrtle Wilson say "had my appendicitis out" rather than "appendix" adds to the delineation of character.

The accumulation of such small changes add up to that Fitzgerald stylistic touch which can only be defined satisfactorily by citing passages. Gatsby's reference to the medal he had received from little Montenegro, for example, was in the galley proof: "Little Montenegro! He lifted up the words and nodded at them—with a faint smile." But when Fitzgerald went over the galleys, he substituted "his" for "a faint" and wrote in that brilliant gloss which now fills out the paragraph: "The smile comprehended Montenegro's troubled history and sympathized with the brave struggles of the Montenegrin people. It appreciated fully the chain of national circumstances which had elicited this tribute from Montenegro's warm little heart."

More often than not in the most heavily revised sections of the galleys, Fitzgerald cut passages, tightened dialogue, and reduced explicit statements in order to heighten the evocative power of his prose. A phrase like Gatsby's "I came here to remember, not to forget," is crossed out to let the passage create the attitude rather than have the phrase spell it out. That final remark of Gatsby's had originally followed this speech: " 'I drift here and there trying to forget the sad thing that happened to me.' He hesitated. 'You'll hear about it this afternoon.' "

ACTION IS CHARACTER, Fitzgerald wrote in his notes for *The Last Tycoon*. His galley proof revisions of *The Great Gatsby* reveal his continuing attention to that precept, particularly in his quickening of the dialogue through which the novel often makes its vital disclosures and confrontations. The truth of Gatsby's connection with Oxford was originally revealed to Nick Carraway in a somewhat flat though detailed conversation with Gatsby in which Gatsby tries to define his feeling for Daisy. Most of that conversation was cut out and the Oxford material worked into the taut dialogue between Tom Buchanan and Gatsby in the Plaza Hotel, which prefaces the story's sweep to its final action.

From almost any of Fitzgerald's original manuscripts, observations like the above can be multiplied to explain the excellence of his style and how that excellence was achieved. Suffice to say here that these observations on *The Great Gatsby* are all drawn from an examination of changes on the galley proofs; they are the final changes which only came after much previous tuning and blending and refining of that superb instrument which was Fitzgerald's style.

Scott Fitzgerald's Criticism of America

Marius Bewley

Critics of Scott Fitzgerald tend to agree that *The Great Gatsby* is some-how a commentary on that elusive phrase, the American dream. The assumption seems to be that Fitzgerald approved. On the contrary, it can be shown that *The Great Gatsby* offers some of the severest and closest criticism of the American dream that our literature affords. Read in this way, Fitzgerald's masterpiece ceases to be a pastoral documentary of the Jazz Age and takes its distinguished place among those great national novels whose profound corrective insights into the nature of American experience are not separable from the artistic form of the novel itself. That is to say, Fitzgerald—at least in this one book—is in a line with the greatest masters of American prose. *The Great Gatsby* embodies a crit-icism of American experience—not of manners, but of a basic historic attitude to life—more radical than anything in James's own assessment of the deficiencies of his country. The theme of *Gatsby* is the withering of the American dream.

Essentially, this phrase represents the romantic enlargement of the possibilities of life on a level at which the material and the spiritual have become inextricably confused. As such, it led inevitably toward the prob-lem that has always confronted American artists dealing with American experience—the problem of determining the hidden boundary in the American vision of life at which the reality ends and the illusion begins. Historically, the American dream is anti-Calvinistic, and believes in the goodness of nature and man. It is accordingly a product of the frontier and the West rather than of the Puritan Tradition. The simultaneous operation of two such attitudes in American life created a tension out of

From *The Sewanee Review*, 62 (1954). Copyright © 1954 by The University of the South.

which much of our greatest art has sprung. Youth of the spirit—perhaps of the body as well—is a requirement of its existence; limit and deprivation are its blackest devils. But it shows an astonishing incapacity to believe in them:

> I join you . . . in branding as cowardly the idea that the human mind is incapable of further advances. This is precisely the doctrine which the present despots of the earth are inculcating, and their friends here re-echoing; and applying especially to religion and politics; "that it is not probable that anything better will be discovered than what was known to our fathers." . . . But thank heaven the American mind is already too much opened to listen to these impostures, and while the art of printing is left to us, science can never be retrograde. . . . To preserve the freedom of the human mind . . . every spirit should be ready to devote itself to martyrdom. . . . But that the enthusiasm which characterizes youth should lift its parricide hands against freedom and science would be such a monstrous phenomenon as I could not place among the possible things in this age and country.

That is the hard kernel, the seed from which the American dream would grow into unpruned luxuriance. Jefferson's voice is not remote from many European voices of his time, but it stands in unique relation to the country to whom he spoke. That attitude was bred into the bone of America, and in various, often distorted, ways, it has lasted. Perhaps that is where the trouble begins, for if these virtues of the American imagination have the elements of greatness in them, they call immediately for discriminating and practical correctives. The reality of such an attitude lies in its faith in life; the illusion lies in the undiscriminating multiplication of its material possibilities.

The Great Gatsby is an exploration of the American dream as it exists in a corrupt period, and it is an attempt to determine that concealed boundary that divides the reality from the illusions. The illusions seem more real than the reality itself. Embodied in the subordinate characters in the novel, they threaten to invade the whole of the picture. On the other hand, the reality is embodied in Gatsby; and as opposed to the hard, tangible illusions, the reality is a thing of the spirit, a promise rather than the possession of a vision, a faith in the half-glimpsed, but hardly understood, possibilities of life. In Gatsby's America, the reality is undefined to itself. It is inarticulate and frustrated. Nick Carraway, Gatsby's friend and Fitzgerald's narrator, says of Gatsby:

> Through all he said, even through his appalling sentimentality, I was reminded of something—an elusive rhythm, a fragment of lost words, that I had heard somewhere a long time ago. For a moment a phrase tried to take shape in my mouth and my lips parted like a dumb man's, as though

there was more struggling upon them than a wisp of startled air. But they made no sound, and what I had almost remembered was incommunicado forever.

This is not pretentious phrase-making performing a vague gesture towards some artificial significance. It is both an evocative and an exact description of that unholy cruel paradox by which the conditions of American history have condemned the grandeur of the aspiration and vision to expend itself in a waste of shame and silence. But that reality is not entirely lost. It ends by redeeming the human spirit, even though it live in a wilderness of illusions, from the cheapness and vulgarity that encompass it. In this novel, the illusions are known and condemned at last simply by the rank complacency with which they are content to be themselves. On the other hand, the reality is in the energy of the spirit's resistance, which may not recognize itself as resistance at all, but which can neither stoop to the illusions nor abide with them when they are at last recognized. Perhaps it is really nothing more than ultimate immunity from the final contamination, but it encompasses the difference between life and death. Gatsby never succeeds in seeing through the sham of his world or his acquaintances very clearly. It is of the essence of his romantic American vision that it should lack the seasoned powers of discrimination. But it invests those illusions with its own faith, and thus it discovers its projected goodness in the frauds of its crippled world. *The Great Gatsby* becomes the acting out of the tragedy of the American vision. It is a vision totally untouched by the scales of values that order life in a society governed by traditional manners; and Fitzgerald knows that although it would be easy to condemn and "place" the illusions by invoking these outside values, to do so would be to kill the reality that lies beyond them, but which can sometimes only be reached through them.

For example, Fitzgerald perfectly understood the inadequacy of Gatsby's romantic view of wealth. But that is not the point. He presents it in Gatsby as a romantic baptism of desire for a reality that stubbornly remains out of his sight. It is as if a savage islander, suddenly touched with Grace, transcended in his prayers and aspirations the grotesque little fetish in which he imagined he discovered the object of his longing. The scene in which Gatsby shows his piles of beautiful imported shirts to Daisy and Nick has been mentioned as a failure of Gatsby's, and so of Fitzgerald's, critical control of values. Actually, the shirts are sacramentals, and it is clear that Gatsby shows them, neither in vanity nor in pride, but with a reverential humility in the presence of some inner vision he cannot consciously grasp, but toward which he desperately struggles in the only way he knows.

In an essay called "Myths for Materialists" Mr. Jacques Barzun once wrote that figures, whether of fact or fiction, insofar as they express destinies, aspirations, attitudes typical of man or particular groups, are invested with a mythical character. In this sense Gatsby is a "mythic" character, and no other word will define him. Not only is he an embodiment (as Fitzgerald makes clear at the outset) of that conflict between illusion and reality at the heart of American life; he is an heroic personification of the American romantic hero, the true heir of the American dream. "There was something gorgeous about him," Nick Carraway says, and although "gorgeous" was a favorite word with the twenties, Gatsby wears it with an archetypal American elegance.

One need not look far in earlier American literature to find his forebears. Here is the description of a young bee hunter from *Col. David Crockett's Exploits and Adventures in Texas*, published in 1836:

> I thought myself alone in the street, where the hush of morning was suddenly broken by a clear, joyful, and musical voice, which sang. . . .
> I turned toward the spot whence the sounds proceeded, and discovered a tall figure leaning against the sign post. His eyes were fixed on the streaks of light in the east, his mind was absorbed, and he was clearly unconscious of anyone being near him. He continued his song in so full and clear a tone, that the street re-echoed. . . .
> I now drew nigh enough to see him distinctly. He was a young man, not more than twenty-two. His figure was light and graceful at the same time that it indicated strength and activity. He was dressed in a hunting shirt, which was made with uncommon neatness, and ornamented tastily with fringe. He held a highly finished rifle in his right hand, and a hunting pouch, covered with Indian ornaments, was slung across his shoulders. His clean shirt collar was open, secured only by a black riband around his neck. His boots were polished, without a soil upon them; and on his head was a neat fur cap, tossed on in a manner which said, "I don't give a d-n," just as plainly as any cap could speak it. I thought it must be some popinjay on a lark, until I took a look at his countenance. It was handsome, bright, and manly. There was no mistake in that face. From the eyes down to the breast he was sunburnt as dark as mahogany while the upper part of his high forehead was as white and polished as marble. Thick clusters of black hair curled from under his cap. I passed on unperceived, and he continued his song. . . .

This young dandy of the frontier, dreaming in the dawn and singing to the morning, is a progenitor of Gatsby. It is because of such a traditional American ancestry that Gatsby's romanticism transcends the limiting glamor of the Jazz Age.

But such a romanticism is not enough to "mythicize" Gatsby. Gatsby, for all his shimmer of representative surfaces, is never allowed to become soiled by the touch of realism. In creating him, Fitzgerald observed as high a decorum of character as a Renaissance playwright: for Gatsby's parents were shiftless and unsuccessful farm people, Gatsby really "sprang from his Platonic conception of himself. He was a son of God—a phrase which, if it means anything, means just that—and he must be about His Father's business, the service of a vast, vulgar, meretricious beauty."

Fitzgerald created Gatsby with a sense of his own election; but the beauty it was in his nature to serve had already been betrayed by history. Even in the midst of the blighted earthly paradise of West Egg, Long Island, Gatsby bore about him the marks of his birth. He is a kind of exiled Duke in disguise. We know him by his bearing, the decorous pattern of his speech. Even his dress invariably touches the imagination: "Gatsby in a white flannel suit, silver shirt, and gold colored tie. . . ." There is something dogmatically Olympic about the combination. After Gatsby's death when his pathetic old father journeys east for the funeral, one feels that he is only the kindly shepherd who once found a baby on the cold hillside.

But so far I have been talking in general terms. This beautiful control of conventions can be studied more closely in the description of Gatsby's party at which (if we except that distant glimpse of him at the end of chapter 1, of which I shall speak later) we encounter him for the first time. We are told later that Gatsby was gifted with a "hint of the unreality of reality, a promise that the rock of the world was founded securely on a fairy's wing." Fitzgerald does not actually let us meet Gatsby face to face until he has concretely created this fantastic world of Gatsby's vision, for it is the element in which we must meet Gatsby if we are to understand his impersonal significance:

> There was music from my neighbor's house through the summer nights. In his blue gardens men and girls came and went like moths among the whisperings and the champagne and the stars. At high tide in the afternoon I watched his guests diving from the tower of his raft, or taking the sun on the hot sand of his beach while his two motor-boats slit the waters of the Sound, drawing aquaplanes over cataracts of foam. On week-ends his Rolls-Royce became an omnibus, bearing parties to and from the city between nine in the morning and long past midnight, while his station wagon scampered like a brisk yellow bug to meet all trains. And on Mondays eight servants, including an extra gardener, toiled all day with mops and scrubbing-brushes and hammers and garden-shears, repairing the ravages of the night before.

The nostalgic poetic quality, which tends to leave one longing for sterner stuff, is, in fact, deceptive. It is Gatsby's ordeal that he must separate the foul dust that floated in the wake of his dreams from the reality of the dream itself: that he must find some vantage point from which he can bring the responsibilities and the possibilities of life into a single focus. But the "ineffable gaudiness" of the world to which Gatsby is committed is a fatal deterrent. Even within the compass of this paragraph we see how the focus has become blurred: how the possibilities of life are conceived of in material terms. But in that heroic list of the vaster luxury items—motor-boats, aquaplanes, private beaches, Rolls-Royces, diving towers—Gatsby's vision maintains its gigantic unreal stature. It imposes a rhythm on his guests which they accept in terms of their own tawdry illusions, having no conception of the compulsion that drives him to offer them the hospitality of his fabulous wealth. They come for their weekends as George Dane in Henry James's *The Great Good Place* went into his dream retreat. But the result is not the same: "on Mondays eight servants, including an extra gardener, toiled all day with mops and scrubbing-brushes and hammers and garden-shears, repairing the ravages of the night before." That is the most important sentence in the paragraph, and despite the fairy-story overtone, it possesses an ironic nuance that rises toward the tragic. And how fine that touch of the extra gardener is—as if Gatsby's guests had made a breach in nature. It completely qualifies the over-fragility of the moths and champagne and blue gardens in the opening sentences.

This theme of the relation of his guests to Gatsby is still further pursued in chapter 4. The cataloguing of American proper names with poetic intention has been an ineffectual cliché in American writing for many generations. But Fitzgerald uses the convention magnificently:

> Once I wrote down on the empty spaces of a time-table the names of those who came to Gatsby's house that summer. It is an old time-table now, disintegrating at its folds, and headed "This schedule in effect July 5th, 1922." But I can still read the gray names, and they will give you a better impression than my generalities of those who accepted Gatsby's hospitality and paid him the subtle tribute of knowing nothing about him.

The names of these guests could have been recorded nowhere else as appropriately as in the margins of a faded timetable. The embodiments of illusions, they are as ephemeral as time itself; but because their illusions represent the distortions and shards of some shattered American dream, the timetable they adorn is "in effect July 5th"—the day following the great national festival when the exhausted holiday crowds, as spent as exploded firecrackers, return to their homes. The list of names which Fitzgerald proceeds to enumerate conjures up with remarkable precision an atmosphere of vulgar American fortunes and vulgar American destinies. Those who are familiar with the social registers, businessmen's directories, and movie magazines of the twenties might be able to analyze the exact way in which Fitzgerald achieves his effect, but it is enough to say here that he shares with Eliot a remarkable clairvoyance in seizing the cultural implications of proper names. After two pages and more, the list ends with the dreamily elegiac close: "All these people came to Gatsby's house in the summer."

Why did they come? There is the answer of the plotted story—the free party, the motor-boats, the private beach, the endless flow of cocktails. But in the completed pattern of the novel one knows that they came for another reason—came blindly and instinctively—illusions in pursuit of a reality from which they have become historically separated, but by which they might alone be completed or fulfilled. And why did Gatsby invite them? As contrasted with them, he alone has a sense of the reality that hovers somewhere out of sight in this nearly ruined American dream; but the reality is unintelligible until he can invest it again with the tangible forms of his world, and relate it to the logic of history. Gatsby and his guests feel a mutual need of each other, but the division in American experience has widened too far, and no party, no hospitality however lavish, can heal the breach. The illusions and the reality go their separate ways. Gatsby stands at the door of his mansion, in one of the most deeply moving and significant paragraphs of the novel, to wish his guests good-bye:

> The caterwauling horns had reached a crescendo and I turned away and cut across the lawn toward home. I glanced back once. A wafer of a moon was shining over Gatsby's house, making the night fine as before, and surviving the laughter and the sound of his still glowing garden. A sudden emptiness seemed to flow now from the windows and the great doors, endowing with complete isolation the figure of the host, who stood on the porch, his hand up in a formal gesture of farewell.

If one turns back to Davy Crockett's description of the elegant young bee hunter, singing while the dawn breaks in the east, and thinks of it in relation with this midnight picture of Gatsby, "his hand up in a formal gesture of farewell," while the last guests depart through the debris of the finished party, the quality of the romanticism seems much the same, but the situation is exactly reversed; and from the latter scene there opens a perspective of profound meaning. Suddenly Gatsby is not merely a likable, romantic hero; he is a creature of myth in whom is incarnated the aspiration and the ordeal of his race.

"Mythic" characters are impersonal. There is no distinction between their public and their private lives. Because they share their meaning with everyone, they have no secrets and no hidden corners into which they can retire for a moment, unobserved. An intimacy so universal stands revealed in a ritual pattern for the inspection and instruction of the race. The "mythic" character can never withdraw from that air which is his existence—that is to say, from that area of consciousness (and hence of publicity) which every individual shares with the members, both living and dead, of his group or race. Gatsby is a "mythic" character in this sense—he has no private life, no meaning or significance that depends on the fulfillment of his merely private destiny, his happiness as an individual in a society of individuals. In a transcendent sense he touches our imaginations, but in this smaller sense—which is the world of the realistic novel—he even fails to arouse our curiosity. At this level, his love affair with Daisy is too easily "placed," a tawdry epic "crush" of no depth or interest in itself. But Gatsby not only remains undiminished by what is essentially the meanness of the affair: his stature grows, as we watch, to the proportions of a hero. We must inquire how Fitzgerald managed this extraordinary achievement.

Daisy Buchanan exists at two well-defined levels in the novel. She is what she is—but she exists also at the level of Gatsby's vision of her. The intelligence of no other important novelist has been as consistently undervalued as Fitzgerald's, and it is hardly surprising that no critic has ever given Fitzgerald credit for his superb understanding of Daisy's vicious emptiness. Even Fitzgerald's admirers regard Daisy as rather a good, if somewhat silly, little thing; but Fitzgerald knew that at its most depraved levels the American dream merges with the American debutante's dream—a thing of deathly hollowness. Fitzgerald faces up squarely to the problem of telling us what Daisy has to offer in a human relationship. At one of Gatsby's fabulous parties—the one to which Daisy brings her husband, Tom Buchanan—Gatsby points out to Daisy and Tom, among the celebrated guests, one particular couple:

> "Perhaps you know that lady," Gatsby indicated a gorgeous, scarcely human orchid of a woman who sat in state under a white-plum tree. Tom and Daisy stared, with that peculiarly unreal feeling that accompanies the recognition of a hitherto ghostly celebrity of the movies.
> "She's lovely," said Daisy.
> "The man bending over her is her director."

Superficially, the scene is highly civilized. One fancies one has seen it in Manet. But in the context we know that it has no reality whatever—the star and her director can get no nearer reality than by rehearsing a scene. Our attention is then taken up by other scenes at the party, but by suddenly returning to this couple after an interval of two pages to make his point, Fitzgerald achieves a curious impression of static or arrested action. We have the feeling that if we walked behind the white-plum tree we should only see the back of a canvas screen:

> Almost the last thing I remember was standing with Daisy and watching the moving-picture director and his Star. They were still under the white-plum tree and their faces were touching except for a pale, thin ray of moonlight between. It occurred to me that he had been very slowly bending toward her all evening to attain this proximity, and even while I watched I saw him stoop one ultimate degree and kiss at her cheek.
> "I like her," said Daisy, "I think she's lovely."
> But the rest offended her—and inarguably, because it wasn't a gesture but an emotion.

Daisy likes the moving-picture actress because she has no substance. She is a gesture that is committed to nothing more real than her own image on the silver screen. She has become a gesture divorced forever from the tiresomeness of human reality. In effect, this passage is Daisy's confession of faith. She virtually announces here what her criteria of human emotions and conduct are. Fitzgerald's illustration of the emptiness of Daisy's character—an emptiness that we see curdling into the viciousness of a monstrous moral indifference as the story unfolds—is drawn with a fineness and depth of critical understanding, and communicated with a force of imagery so rare in modern American writing, that it is almost astonishing that he is often credited with giving in to those very qualities which *The Great Gatsby* so effectively excoriates.

But what is the basis for the mutual attraction between Daisy and Gatsby? In Daisy's case the answer is simple. We remember that Nick Carraway has described Gatsby's personality as an "unbroken series of successful gestures." Superficially, Daisy finds in Gatsby, or thinks she finds, that safety from human reality which the empty gesture implies. What she fails to realize is that Gatsby's gorgeous gesturings are the reflex of an aspiration toward the possibilities of life, and this is something entirely different from those vacant images of romance and sophistication that fade so easily into the nothingness from which they came. But in a sense, Daisy is safe enough from the reality she dreads. The true question is not what Gatsby sees in Daisy, but the direction he takes from her, what he sees *beyond* her; and that has, despite the immaturity intrinsic in Gatsby's vision, an element of grandeur in it. For Gatsby, Daisy does not exist in herself. She is the green light that signals him into the heart of his ultimate vision. *Why* she should have this evocative power over Gatsby is a question Fitzgerald faces beautifully and successfully as he recreates that milieu of uncritical snobbishness and frustrated idealism—monstrous fusion—which is the world in which Gatsby is compelled to live.

Fitzgerald, then, has a sure control when he defines the quality of this love affair. He shows it in itself as vulgar and specious. It has no possible interest in its own right, and if it did have the pattern of the novel would be ruined. Our imaginations would be fettered in those details and interests which would detain us on the narrative level where the affair works itself out as human history, and Gatsby would lose his "mythic" quality. But the economy with which Gatsby is presented, the formal and boldly drawn structural lines of his imagination, lead us at once to a level where it is obvious that Daisy's significance in the story lies in her failure to represent the objective correlative of Gatsby's vision. And at the same time, Daisy's wonderfully representative quality as a creature of the Jazz Age relates her personal failure to the larger failure of Gatsby's society to satisfy his need. In fact, Fitzgerald never allows Daisy's failure to become a human or personal one. He maintains it with sureness on a symbolic level where it is identified with and reflects the failure of Gatsby's decadent American world. There is a famous passage in which Gatsby sees Daisy as an embodiment of the glamor of wealth. Nick Carraway is speaking first to Gatsby:

> "She's got an indiscreet voice," I remarked. "It's full of—" I hesitated.
> "Her voice is full of money," he said suddenly.
> That was it. I'd never understood before. It was full of money—that was the inexhaustible charm that rose and fell in it, the jingle of it, the cymbals' song of it. . . . High in a white palace the king's daughter, the golden girl . . .

Gatsby tries to build up the inadequacy of each value by the support of the other; but united they fall as wretchedly short of what he is seeking as each does singly. Gatsby's gold and Gatsby's girl belong to the fairy story in which the Princess spins whole rooms of money from skeins of wool. In the fairy story, the value never lies in the gold but in something beyond. And so it is in this story. For Gatsby, Daisy is only the promise of fulfillment that lies beyond the green light that burns all night on her dock.

This green light that is visible at night across the bay from the windows and lawn of Gatsby's house is the central symbol in the book. Significantly, our first glimpse of Gatsby at the end of chapter 1 is related to it. Nick Carraway, whose modest bungalow in West Egg stands next to Gatsby's mansion, returning from an evening at the Buchanans', while lingering on the lawn for a final moment under the stars, becomes aware that he is not alone:

> Fifty feet away a figure had emerged from the shadow of my neighbor's mansion and was standing with his hands in his pockets regarding the

silver pepper of the stars. Something in his leisurely movements and the secure position of his feet upon the lawn suggested that it was Mr. Gatsby himself, come out to determine what share was his of our local heavens.

I decided to call to him. . . . But I didn't . . . for he gave a sudden intimation that he was content to be alone—he stretched out his arms toward the dark water in a curious way, and, as far as I was from him, I could have sworn he was trembling. Involuntarily I glanced seaward—and distinguished nothing except a single green light, minute and far away, that might have been the end of a dock. When I looked once more for Gatsby he had vanished, and I was alone again in the unquiet darkness.

It is hardly too much to say that the whole being of Gatsby exists only in relation to what the green light symbolizes. This first sight we have of Gatsby is a ritualistic tableau that literally contains the meaning of the completed book, although the full meaning of what is implicit in the symbol reveals itself slowly, and is only finally rounded out on the last page. We have a fuller definition of what the green light means in its particular, as opposed to its universal, signification in chapter 5. Gatsby is speaking to Daisy as they stand at one of the windows of his mansion:

"If it wasn't for the mist we could see your home across the bay," said Gatsby. "You always have a green light that burns all night at the end of your dock."

Daisy put her arm through his abruptly, but he seemed absorbed in what he had just said. Possibly it had occurred to him that the colossal significance of that light had now vanished forever. Compared to the great distance that had separated him from Daisy it had seemed very near to her, almost touching her. It had seemed as close as a star to the moon. Now it was again a green light on a dock. His count of enchanted objects had diminished by one.

Some might object to this symbolism on the grounds that it is easily vulgarized—as A. J. Cronin has proved. But if studied carefully in its full context it represents a convincing achievement. The tone or pitch of the symbol is exactly adequate to the problem it dramatizes. Its immediate function is that it signals Gatsby into his future, away from the cheapness of his affair with Daisy which he has vainly tried (and desperately continues trying) to create in the image of his vision. The green light is successful because, apart from its visual effectiveness as it gleams across the bay, it embodies the profound naiveté of Gatsby's sense of the future, while simultaneously suggesting the historicity of his hope. This note of historicity is not fully apparent at this point, of course. The symbol occurs several times, and most notably at the end:

Gatsby believed in the green light, the orgastic future that year by year recedes before us. It eluded us then, but that's no matter—tomorrow we will run faster, stretch out our arms farther. . . . And one fine morning—

So we beat on, boats against the current, borne back ceaselessly into the past.

Thus the American dream, whose superstitious valuation of the future began in the past, gives the green light through which alone the American returns to his traditional roots, paradoxically retreating into the pattern of history while endeavoring to exploit the possibilities of the future. There is a suggestive echo of the past in Gatsby's sense of Daisy. He had known her, and fallen in love with her, five years before the novel opens. During that long interval while they had disappeared from each other's sight, Daisy has become a legend in Gatsby's memory, a part of his private past which (as a "mythic" character) he assimilates into the pattern of that historic past through which he would move into the historic future. But the legendary Daisy, meeting her after five years, has dimmed a little in luster:

> "And she doesn't understand," he said. "She used to be able to understand. We'd sit for hours—"
> He broke off and began to walk up and down a desolate path of fruit rinds and discarded favors and crushed flowers.
> "I wouldn't ask too much of her," I ventured. "You can't repeat the past."
> "Can't repeat the past?" he cried incredulously. "Why of course you can!"
> He looked around him wildly, as if the past were lurking here in the shadow of his house, just out of reach of his hand.

By such passages Fitzgerald dramatizes Gatsby's symbolic role. The American dream, stretched between a golden past and a golden future, is always betrayed by a desolate present—a moment of fruit rinds and discarded favors and crushed flowers. Imprisoned in his present, Gatsby belongs even more to the past than to the future. His aspirations have been rehearsed, and his tragedy suffered, by all the generations of Americans who have gone before. His sense of the future, of the possibilities of life, he has learned from the dead.

If we return to the passage in which, linked arm in arm, Gatsby and Daisy stand at the window looking toward the green light across the bay, it may be possible to follow a little more sympathetically that quality of disillusion which begins to creep into Gatsby's response to life. It does not happen because of the impoverished elements of his practical romance: it happens because Gatsby is incapable of compromising with his inner vision. The imagery of this particular passage, as I suggested, is gauged to meet the requirements of Gatsby's young romantic dream. But two pages later Fitzgerald takes up the theme of Gatsby's struggle against disenchantment once again, and this time in an imagery that suggests how much he had learned from *The Waste Land*:

> When Klipspringer had played "The Love Nest" he turned around on the bench and searched unhappily for Gatsby in the gloom.
> "I'm all out of practice, you see. I told you I couldn't play. I'm all out of prac—"
> "Don't talk so much, old sport," commanded Gatsby. "Play!"
>
> > *In the morning,*
> > *In the evening,*
> > *Ain't we got fun—*
>
> Outside the wind was loud and there was a faint flow of thunder along the Sound. All the lights were going on in West Egg now; the electric trains, men-carrying, were plunging home through the rain from New York. It was the hour of a profound human change, and excitement was generating on the air.
>
> > *One thing's sure and nothing's surer*
> > *The rich get richer and the poor get—children.*
> > *In the meantime,*
> > *In between time—*
>
> As I went over to say good-by I saw that the expression of bewilderment had come back into Gatsby's face, as though a faint doubt had occurred to him as to the quality of his present happiness. Almost five years! There must have been moments even that afternoon when Daisy tumbled short of his dreams—not through her own fault, but because of the colossal vitality of his illusion. It had gone beyond her, beyond everything. He had thrown himself into it with a creative passion, adding to it all the time, decking it out with every bright feather that drifted his way. No amount of fire or freshness can challenge what a man can store up in his ghostly heart.

In view of such writing it is absurd to argue that Fitzgerald's art was a victim of his own attraction to the Jazz Age. The snatches of song that Klipspringer sings evoke the period with an immediacy that is necessary if we are to understand the peculiar poignancy of Gatsby's ordeal. But the songs are more than evocative. They provide the ironic musical prothalamion for Gatsby's romance, and as Gatsby listens to them an intimation of the practical truth presses in on him. The recognition is heightened poetically by that sense of the elements, the faint flow of thunder along the Sound, which forms the background of those artificial little tunes. And it is not odd that this evocation of the outdoor scene, while Klipspringer pounds at the piano inside, sustains in the imagination the image of that green light, symbol of Gatsby's faith, which is burning across the bay. This scene draws on the "violet hour" passage from "The Fire Sermon" in which "the human engine waits/Like a taxi throbbing waiting. . . ." It is the hour of a profound human change, and in the faint stirrings of Gatsby's recognition there is for a moment, perhaps, a possibility of his escape. But the essence of the American dream whose tragedy Gatsby is enacting is that it lives in a past and a future that never existed, and is helpless in the present that does.

Gatsby's opposite number in the story is Daisy's husband, Tom Buchanan, and Gatsby's stature—his touch of doomed but imperishable spiritual beauty, if I may call it so—is defined by his contrast with Tom. In many ways they are analogous in their characteristics—just sufficiently so to point up the differences. For example, their youth is an essential quality of them both. But Tom Buchanan was "one of those men who reach such an acute limited excellence at twenty-one that everything afterward savors of anti-climax." Even his body—"a body capable of enormous leverage"—was "a cruel body." In the description of Tom we are left physically face to face with a scion of those ruthless generations who raised up the great American fortunes, and who now live in uneasy arrogant leisure on their brutal acquisitions. But Gatsby's youth leaves an impression of interminability. Its climax is always in the future, and it gives rather than demands. Its energy is not in its body, but in its spirit, and meeting Gatsby for the first time, one seizes, as Nick Carraway did, this impression in his smile:

> It was one of those rare smiles with a quality of eternal reassurance in it, that you may come across four or five times in life. It faced—or seemed to face—the whole external world for an instant, and then concentrated on *you* with an irresistible prejudice in your favor. It understood you just as far as you wanted to be understood, believed in you as you would like to believe in yourself, and assured you that it had precisely the impression of you that, at your best, you hoped to convey. Precisely at that point it vanished—and I was looking at an elegant young rough-neck, a year or two over thirty, whose elaborate formality of speech just missed being absurd.

This passage is masterly in the way in which it presents Gatsby to us less as an individual than as a projection, or mirror, of our ideal selves. To do that is the function of all "mythic" characters. Gatsby's youth is not simply a matter of three decades that will quickly multiply themselves into four or five. It is a quality of faith and hope that may be betrayed by history, may be killed by society, but that no exposure to the cynical turns of time can reduce to the compromises of age.

Again, Gatsby and Tom are alike in the possession of a certain sentimentality, but Tom Buchanan's is based on depraved self-pity. He is never more typical than when coaxing himself to tears over a half-finished box of dog biscuits that recalls a drunken and illicit day from his past, associated in memory with his dead mistress. His self-pity is functional. It is sufficient to condone his most criminal acts in his own eyes as long as the crimes are not imputable. But Gatsby's sentimentality exists in the difficulty of expressing, in the phrases and symbols provided by his decadent society, the reality that lies at the heart of his aspiration. "So he waited, listening for a moment longer to the tuning fork that had been struck upon a star"—Gatsby's sentimentality (if it *is* sentimentality, and I rather doubt it) is as innocent as that. It has nothing of self-pity or indulgence in it—it is all aspiration and goodness; and it must be remembered that Fitzgerald himself is *outside* Gatsby's vocabulary, using it with great mastery to convey the poignancy of the situation.

Tom Buchanan and Gatsby represent antagonistic but historically related aspects of America. They are related as the body and the soul when a mortal barrier has risen up between them. Tom Buchanan is virtually Gatsby's murderer in the end, but the crime that he commits by proxy is only a symbol of his deeper spiritual crime against Gatsby's inner vision. Gatsby's guilt, insofar as it exists, is radical failure—a failure of the critical faculty that seems to be an inherent part of the American dream—to understand that Daisy is as fully immersed in the destructive element of the American world as Tom himself. After Daisy, while driving Gatsby's white automobile, has killed Mrs. Wilson and, implicitly at least, left Gatsby to shoulder the blame, Nick Carraway gives us a crucial insight into the spiritual affinity of the Buchanan couple, drawing together in their callous selfishness in a moment of guilt and crisis:

> Daisy and Tom were sitting opposite each other at the kitchen table, with a plate of cold fried chicken between them, and two bottles of ale. He was talking intently across the table at her, and in his earnestness his hand had fallen upon and covered her own. Once in a while she looked up at him and nodded in agreement.
> They weren't happy, and neither of them had touched the chicken or the ale—and yet they weren't unhappy either. There was an unmistakable air of natural intimacy about the picture, and anybody would have said that they were conspiring together.

They instinctively seek out each other because each recognizes the other's strength in the corrupt spiritual element they inhabit.

There is little point in tracing out in detail the implications of the action any further, although it could be done with an exactness approaching allegory. That it is not allegory is owing to the fact that the pattern emerges from the fullness of Fitzgerald's living experience of his own society and time. In the end the most that can be said is that *The Great Gatsby* is a dramatic affirmation in fictional terms of the American spirit in the midst of an American world that denies the soul. Gatsby exists in, and for, that affirmation alone.

When, at the end, not even Gatsby can hide his recognition of the speciousness of his dream any longer, the discovery is made in universalizing terms that dissolve Daisy into the larger world she has stood for in Gatsby's imagination:

> He must have looked up at an unfamiliar sky through frightening leaves and shivered as he found what a grotesque thing a rose is and how raw the sunlight was upon the scarcely created grass. A new world, material without being real, where poor ghosts, breathing dreams like air, drifted fortuitously about. . . .

"A new world, material without being real." Paradoxically, it was Gatsby's dream that conferred reality upon the world. The reality was in his faith in the goodness of creation, and in the possibilities of life. That these possibilities were intrinsically related to such romantic components limited and distorted his dream, and finally left it helpless in the face of the Buchanans, but it did not corrupt it. When the dream melted, it knocked the prop of reality from under the universe, and face to face with the physical substance at last, Gatsby realized that the illusion was *there*—there where Tom and Daisy, and generations of small-minded, ruthless Americans had found it—in the dreamless, visionless complacency of mere matter, substance without form. After this recognition, Gatsby's death is only a symbolic formality, for the world into which his mere body had been born rejected the gift he had been created to embody—the traditional dream from which alone it could awaken into life.

As the novel closes, the experience of Gatsby and his broken dream explicitly becomes the focus of that historic dream for which he stands. Nick Carraway is speaking:

> Most of the big shore places were closed now and there were hardly any lights except the shadowy, moving glow of a ferryboat across the Sound. And as the moon rose higher the inessential houses began to melt away until gradually I became aware of the old island here that flowered once for Dutch sailors' eyes—a fresh, green breast of the new world. Its vanished trees, the trees that had once made way for Gatsby's house, had once pandered in whispers to the last and greatest of all human dreams; for a transitory enchanted moment man must have held his breath in the presence of this continent, compelled into an aesthetic contemplation he nei-

ther understood nor desired, face to face for the last time in history with
something commensurate to his capacity for wonder.

It is fitting that this, like so many of the others in *Gatsby*, should be a
moonlight scene, for the history and the romance are one. Gatsby fades
into the past forever to take his place with the Dutch sailors who had
chosen their moment in time so much more happily than he.

We recognize that the great achievement of this novel is that it
manages, while poetically evoking a sense of the goodness of that early
dream, to offer the most damaging criticism of it in American literature.
The astonishing thing is that the criticism—if indictment wouldn't be
the better word—manages to be part of the tribute. Gatsby, the "mythic"
embodiment of the American dream, is shown to us in all his immature
romanticism. His insecure grasp of social and human values, his lack of
critical intelligence and self-knowledge, his blindness to the pitfalls that
surround him in American society, his compulsive optimism, are realized
in the text with rare assurance and understanding. And yet the very
grounding of these deficiencies is Gatsby's goodness and faith in life, his
compelling desire to realize all the possibilities of existence, his belief
that we can have an Earthly Paradise populated by Buchanans. A great
part of Fitzgerald's achievement is that he suggests effectively that these
terrifying deficiencies are not so much the private deficiencies of Gatsby,
but are deficiencies inherent in contemporary manifestations of the
American vision itself—a vision no doubt admirable, but stupidly de-
fenseless before the equally American world of Tom and Daisy. Gatsby's
deficiencies of intelligence and judgment bring him to his tragic death—
a death that is spiritual as well as physical. But the more important
question that faces us through our sense of the immediate tragedy is
where they have brought America.

Two Versions of the Hero

David Parker

Together with many other works of fiction, *The Great Gatsby* is often interpreted as a parable of disenchantment with the American Dream. Such it may be, but the experience of strong idealism, boundless optimism, and a sense of destiny, all terminated by the failure of actuality to measure up to hope, is not an experience peculiar to citizens of the U.S.A. *The Great Gatsby* is a masterpiece not by American standards alone.

I propose to examine the novel against the background of English literature. It makes sense to see Fitzgerald, a student of English at Princeton, as an Anglo-Saxon rather than purely American writer, and it seems to me that the notable position of the novel in the history of Western sensibility is best brought out by studying it against the older tradition. Such a method, incidentally, helps define the American Dream more exactly.

There are in English literature two chief versions of the hero. Often they share characteristics, and sometimes a hero is a blend of the two, but there is a tendency for polarisation in one direction or the other, towards distinct patterns of behaviour and character. The first kind of hero is the one whose prototype we find in mediaeval romance and ancient epic: an idealist, loyal to some transcending object, and relentless in his quest for it. He seeks honour, love, or the Sangreal, and he affects the reader with all the potency of myth. The second kind, though doubtless developed from the first, is in sharp contrast. If he has a quest, it is essentially an inward one. Circumstances compel him to explore his own being, to discover, and perhaps to modify, his own identity. He is typified by the hero of the novel of sentimental education.

From *English Studies* 54, no.1 (February 1973). Copyright © 1973 by Swets & Zeitlinger B. V., Amsterdam.

Versions of the hero roughly corresponding to these two are to be found in American literature. Philip Rahv, in his witty essay on "Paleface and Redskin" in American literature, asks the reader to consider "the immense contrast between the drawing-room fictions of Henry James and the open-air poems of Walt Whitman." The dichotomy suggested by this contrast is a serious one, he declares, "a dichotomy between experience and consciousness—a dissociation between energy and sensibility, between conduct and theories of conduct, between life conceived as an opportunity and life conceived as a discipline." Paleface writers tend naturally to write about paleface heroes, redskin writers about redskin heroes. "The typical American writer," says Rahv, "has so far shown himself incapable of escaping the blight of one-sidedness: of achieving that mature control which permits the balance of impulse with sensitiveness, of natural power with philosophical depth."

The achievement of *The Great Gatsby* it seems to me, is in the profoundly satisfying way Fitzgerald manages to include both versions of the hero in one vision, balancing each against the other, and avoiding "the blight of one-sidedness." Nor, it seems to me, does Fitzgerald thus merely correct a flaw in American letters. His achievement is greater than that. He dramatizes the dilemma of Western twentieth-century man, wavering between energy and sensibility. These terms are embarrassingly wide and vague, perhaps, yet such is the significance of the novel, one hesitates to use narrower, more finical terms. The text, however, unlike the slipshod terms we may use to describe it, does not embarrass in the least.

It has often been observed that Gatsby is in the line of the heroes of romance. "He had committed himself to the following of a grail," Nick Carraway tells us. It is more profitable, I think, to compare Gatsby, not with the heroes of mediaeval romance, but with a more recent version of the same figure, so that we can detect the tradition modifying itself on a smaller time-scale. Fitzgerald's treatment of Gatsby seems to me to invite comparison with Browning's treatment of his hero in "Childe Roland to the Dark Tower Came." Here we see one advantage of studying *The Great Gatsby* against the background of English literature. The knight errant, as such, was still a potent figure for the nineteenth-century English writer and his audience, whereas for their American counterparts, as we see from the writings of Twain for instance, he was a figure of fun. Gatsby is preposterous, but there is something admirable in his chivalrous idealism as well. Fitzgerald manages to generate for Gatsby a kind of wondering respect.

Both Gatsby and Childe Roland pursue their quests in an atmosphere of lies, suspicion, and ambiguity. Gatsby's absurdity inclines the reader to doubt his promise of "God's own truth," and by chapter 6, like Nick, he has "reached the point of believing everything and nothing" about Gatsby, Gatsby's family, Gatsby's career, and Gatsby's affairs. "Childe Roland" opens with uncertainty:

> My first thought was, he lied in every word,
>   That hoary cripple, with malicious eye
>   Askance to watch the workings of his lie
> On mine, and mouth scarce able to afford
> Suppression of the glee that pursed and scored
>   Its edge at one more victim gained thereby.

The cripple turns out to have told the truth, though, and so in many instances does Gatsby.

The great difference is that Fitzgerald's hero is himself suspect, whereas Browning's only moves in a world where suspicion is necessary. This difference marks the changing role of the romantic hero. In the eighteen-fifties it was possible to believe that a heroic quest might bear fruit. The world seemed hostile and malicious, the goal enigmatic—the Dark Tower is ugly and inscrutable—but nevertheless, the hero might retain his integrity and confront his destiny. Fitzgerald writes for a different era, one which suspects the very possibility of such a quest. Gatsby can neither maintain his integrity unscathed, nor find an ideal "commensurate to his capacity for wonder." He has to be content with Daisy, careless, fallible, and treacherous.

Neither Childe Roland nor Gatsby are deterred by delay or the prospect of failure. Finding himself at last within reach of the Dark Tower, Childe Roland meditates:

> For, what with my whole world-wide wandering,
>   What with my search drawn out thro' years, my hope
>   Dwindling into a ghost not fit to cope
> With that obstreperous joy success would bring,
> I hardly tried now to rebuke the spring
>   My heart made, finding failure in its scope.
>
> (st. iv)

Gatsby is no less tenacious, loving Daisy unswervingly for five years, despite their separation and her marriage. When the prospect of reunion is near, his demand is that she should say to her husband, "I never loved you," no less. But once again there is a difference. Childe Roland admits the possibility of failure, but Browning cuts his poem off short before the contest is decided. It is enough that his hero should confront his destiny undeterred: "Dauntless the slug-horn to my lips I set / And blew. *'Childe*

Roland to the Dark Tower came.' " Gatsby too is dauntless, but absurdly so. He cannot conceive failure, and in a sense fails less than the image he chose to embody his dreams. Even this, however, he does not recognize, keeping a "sacred" vigil outside Daisy's house after she has revealed herself all too humanly weak. To Browning's generation heroism appeared difficult; to Fitzgerald's it appears absurd.

Both Childe Roland and Gatsby cross symbolic waste lands in their quests. Much of the poem is taken up with descriptions of this sort:

> So on I went. I think I never saw
>   Such starved ignoble nature; nothing throve:
>   For flowers—as well expect a cedar grove!
> But cockle, spurge, according to their law
> Might propagate their kind, with none to awe,
>   You'd think: a burr had been a treasure-trove.
>
> No! penury, inertness, and grimace,
>   In some strange sort, were the land's portion. "See
>   Or shut your eyes"—said Nature peevishly—
> "It nothing skills: I cannot help my case:
> The Judgment's fire alone can cure this place,
>   Calcine its clods and set my prisoners free."
>
>   (sts. x-xi)

Fitzgerald's waste land is just as barren:

> About half-way between West Egg and New York the motor road hastily joins the railroad and runs beside it for a quarter of a mile, so as to shrink away from a certain desolate area of land. This is a valley of ashes—a fantastic farm where ashes grow like wheat into ridges and hills and grotesque gardens; where ashes take the forms of houses and chimneys and rising smoke and, finally, with a transcendent effort, of ash-grey men, who move dimly and already crumbling through the powdery air. Occasionally a line of grey cars crawls along an invisible track, gives out a ghastly creak, and comes to a rest, and immediately the ash-grey men swarm up with leaden spades and stir up an impenetrable cloud, which screens their obscure operations from your sight.
>
> But above the grey land and the spasms of bleak dust which drift endlessly over it, you perceive, after a moment, the eyes of Doctor T. J. Eckleburg. The eyes of Doctor T. J. Eckleburg are blue and gigantic—their retinas are one yard high. They look out of no face, but instead, from a pair of enormous yellow spectacles which pass over a non-existent nose. Evidently some wild wag of an oculist set them there to fatten his practice in the borough of Queens, and then sank down himself into eternal blindness, or forgot them and moved away. But his eyes, dimmed a little by many paintless days, under sun and rain, brood on over the solemn dumping ground.

The image of the waste land was as much a possession of the Victorian sensibility as it is of the modern. For both it performs a complex symbolic function, as we see in these examples. It reminds us of the squalor and destructiveness of industrial civilization. Fitzgerald's "line of grey cars" has the same effect on the reader as the terrible machine of Browning's poem:

> What bad use was that engine for, that wheel,
> Or brake, not wheel—that harrow fit to reel
> Men's bodies out like silk?
>
> (st. xxiv)

The waste land suggests a withdrawal of value and significance from the world of human affairs. Nature herself, in Browning's poem, explains the predicament: providence is external, remote; only the Last Judgment will set things right. In the novel, all that remains is a ghastly parody of providence. Looking at the faceless eyes of Doctor T. J. Eckleburg, the demented Wilson mutters, "You may fool me, but you can't fool God!" His surprised neighbour has to tell him, "That's an advertisement."

The waste land dramatizes for us the way in which society dwarfs and obscures the efforts of individuals, giving them the appearance of perversion. The inhabitants of Browning's "grey plain" are evident only in the trace of their struggles:

> What made those holes and rents
> In the dock's harsh swarth leaves—bruised as to baulk
> All hope of greenness?
>
> (st. xii)

> Who were the strugglers, what war did they wage
> Whose savage trample thus could pad the dank
> Soil to a plash?
>
> (st. xxii)

Similarly, "the ash-grey men" of Fitzgerald's "grey land" raise "an impenetrable cloud, which screens their obscure operations from your sight." Cruelty, suffering and violent death are the real business of the waste land, we learn. The "stiff blind horse" Childe Roland encounters "must be wicked to deserve such pain" (st. xiv). Fording a stream, the Childe fears to set his foot "upon a dead man's cheek" (st. xxi). The Wilsons mentally torture each other on Fitzgerald's waste land, and it is there that Myrtle Wilson is killed by the "death car." All these things point towards the malignity of the contemporary environment; others towards its sterility. Weeds scarcely grow on Browning's waste land, and the ashes on Fitzgerald's mock the beholder by mimicking in ashen shapes wheat, gardens and human habitations.

The Childe and Gatsby both move in worlds in which corruption is the norm. Childe Roland laments the failure of "the Band," all those who sought the Dark Tower; laments Cuthbert, fallen through "one night's disgrace," and Giles, "the soul of honour," at last hanged, "Poor traitor, spit upon and cursed." As he confronts his destiny before the Dark Tower, the Childe sees all around him the shapes of his lost and fallen peers, "met / To view the last" of him. In Gatsby's world it is less the fall from honour that is striking than the failure to attain honour. Gatsby's guests slander him; his colleagues are typified by Mr. Wolfsheim who fixed the World Series in 1919; and he is despised by the despicable Tom Buchanan. Childe Roland's end is celebrated with some ceremony by the shades of his disgraced companions. At Gatsby's funeral, however, his former companions are conspicuously absent. For Browning even failure and disgrace have some dignity, but Gatsby's shabby acquaintances are to the end cowardly and ungenerous.

The Childe and Gatsby are finally alike in sharing the courage to believe in the value of the objects of their quests. Childe Roland is prepared for the Tower's unimpressiveness:

> The round squat turret, blind as the fool's heart,
>   Built of brown stone, without a counterpart
> In the whole world.
>
> (st. xxxi)

But he and other members of "The Band" know its value, know its uniqueness. Gatsby's courage is similar, but of a different order. He recognizes the danger of making Daisy the embodiment of his dreams:

> The quiet lights in the houses were humming out into the darkness and there was a stir and bustle among the stars. Out of the corner of his eye Gatsby saw that the blocks of the sidewalks really formed a ladder and mounted to a secret place above the trees—he could climb to it, if he climbed alone, and once there he could suck on the pap of life, gulp down the incomparable milk of wonder.

". . . if he climbed alone": Gatsby could revel with impunity as a solitary dreamer, but courageously he projects his dream onto actuality:

> His heart beat faster and faster as Daisy's white face came up to his own. He knew that when he kissed this girl, and forever wed his unutterable visions to her perishable breath, his mind would never romp again like

the mind of God. So he waited, listening for a moment longer to the tuning-fork that had been struck upon a star. Then he kissed her. At her lips' touch she blossomed for him like a flower and the incarnation was complete.

Value really does reside in the object of the Childe's quest, proportional to his expectations. The tower is ugly, but unique. Disaster is threatened only by its magnitude and mystery, by the Childe's not being adequate to its challenge. Disaster comes to Gatsby because Daisy is not adequate to his dreams. Once more we notice the changing role of the romantic hero. Browning's generation were willing to accept the proposition that he could discover value, albeit with difficulty, in the external world. Fitzgerald's felt that value, more often than not, had to be created by the individual, as best he could.

Nick Carraway, the narrator, is the other sort of hero in *The Great Gatsby*, the sort whose sentimental education is advanced. Though detailed comparison is unnecessary in this case, it is worth remarking that Nick in many respects resembles Lockwood, the narrator of *Wuthering Heights*. Both have obvious deficiencies, as men and as tellers of the particular story, but both, through contemplating the astonishing actions and strange passions of others, learn enough at least to begin the correction of those deficiencies. Both come to contemplate with sympathy that which before they could not, or would not, understand.

As he tells us himself, Nick is slow-thinking. He does not learn immediately from his experiences with Gatsby, but slowly, reluctantly, and in retrospect. At the beginning of the novel he tells us, "When I came back from the East last autumn [after Gatsby's death] I felt that I wanted the world to be in uniform and at a sort of moral attention forever; I wanted no more riotous excursions with privileged glimpses into the human heart." Nick's slowness in learning gives an added touch of plausibility to his narration, and makes it very much more dramatic for the reader, who sees him, in the course of the novel, gradually coming to a realization of what his experiences may teach him. This initial response he describes betrays the very deficiency in his character he learns to correct: Nick wants the world and the people in it to be cleaner and simpler than they really are. He values honesty, self-sufficiency, and sticking to the rules—all good things to value, but not in themselves enough. Nick at first is cold hearted and reluctant to recognize the complexity of human beings.

His narration starts like this:

> In my younger and more vulnerable years my father gave me some advice
> that I've been turning over in my mind ever since.

"Whenever you feel like criticizing anyone," he told me, "just remember that all the people in this world haven't had the advantages that
you've had."

Sound enough advice. It is reflections of this sort that help Nick eventually to appreciate Gatsby. But it is advice that provides a rationale as
much for cold-heartedness as it does for sympathy. "Reserving judgments," says Nick, "is a matter of infinite hope," but it is a niggling sort
of hope, compared with Gatsby's "extraordinary gift for hope." One of
the stories Nick tells in *The Great Gatsby* is the story of how he was
able to reach his final judgment on Gatsby:

No—Gatsby turned out all right at the end; it is what preyed on Gatsby,
what foul dust floated in the wake of his dreams that temporarily closed
out my interest in the abortive sorrows and short-winded elations of men.

Nick at first is reluctant to come to terms with the "foul dust."

Like his father's advice, Nick's family background as a whole, well-
established, well-to-do, Middle Western, is both an advantage and a disadvantage in his sentimental education. It gives him a secure sense of
identity and a moral standpoint, but also a moral retreat to which he
may withdraw from the unfamiliar. In the first chapter Nick is ironical
at the expense of "the secret griefs of wild, unknown men," and takes
comfort in his father's maxim that "a sense of the fundamental decencies
is parcelled out unequally at birth." It is not until the last that he reflects
how easy it is to be "a little complacent from growing up in the Carraway
house in a city where dwellings are still called through decades by a
family's name." Admittedly, Nick has always made himself accessible
to the "wild, unknown men," but more out of habit and the respect he
has for his self-image than anything else. "Frequently," he tells us, "I
have feigned sleep, preoccupation, or a hostile levity when I realized by
some unmistakable sign that an intimate revelation was quivering on
the horizon." Nick wisely does not return to the West until he has
sustained the shocks the East gives to his complacency. Only then is he
able knowingly to embrace the West's values.

Nick's Western background, perhaps, contributes to the exaggerated
value he puts on self-sufficiency. "Life is much more successfully looked
at from a single window, after all," he says. But it is a statement imbued
with the irony Nick adopts when reviewing ideas he has discarded.
Gatsby tries looking at life through a single window, with lamentable
results. Tom Buchanan, Daisy's husband, seeks to interpret life like a
football game, and Tom is not admirable. The success that arises from
looking at life through a single window is of the sort that confers on the

individual a pleasing style, but no readiness to judge and sympathize with the unfamiliar and unexpected. Until he learns otherwise, Nick admires Jordan Baker, "this clean hard limited person, who dealt in universal scepticism." "Almost any exhibition of complete self-sufficiency," he admits, "draws a stunned tribute from me."

Until he learns otherwise, Nick shares with Jordan Baker more moral inclinations than he cares to admit. Like her, though less pronouncedly, he tends to feel safer "on a plane where any divergence from a code would be thought impossible." He is in fact something of a prig. Many men who fought in the world wars returned to civilian life nostalgic for the moral simplicity of army life, and Nick is one of them. He reveals his priggish impulses in the account he gives of his first visit to the Buchanans' house. When he learns that it is Tom's mistress on the telephone, Nick's response is characteristic: "To a certain temperament the situation might have seemed intriguing—my own instinct was to telephone immediately for the police." Nick is without sympathy for the way the Buchanans cope with their marital problems: "I was confused and a little disgusted as I drove away. It seemed to me that the thing for Daisy to do was to rush out of the house, child in arms—but apparently there were no such intentions in her head." These statements are not free from Nick's self-mocking irony. That is what redeems them. But they do indicate a certain unfeigned inflexibility of sympathy.

Nick prides himself on his honesty: "Every one suspects himself of at least one of the cardinal virtues, and this is mine: I am one of the few honest people that I have ever known." He is indeed candid, and refrains from telling lies: in that rests the value of his narration. But Nick's honesty seems almost insignificant compared with Gatsby's peculiar dishonesty. Like any virtue, honesty can be used negatively, to narrow and limit sympathy. Gatsby was dishonest with himself and others; his personality was merely "an unbroken series of successful gestures," and yet "there was something gorgeous about him, some heightened sensitivity to the promises of life." The limitations of Nick's honesty are exposed in his reactions to his discovery that Jordan Baker is "incurably dishonest." "It made no difference to me," says Nick. "Dishonesty in a woman is a thing you never blame deeply—I was casually sorry, and then I forgot." Nick wears his honesty for adornment, and to simplify things (it enables him to disapprove of Gatsby for instance). It is not something he values absolutely.

He boasts of his honesty in the conduct of his love affairs. Three of Nick's girls are mentioned in the novel. One is the girl to whom, so Tom and Daisy have heard, Nick is engaged. He denies this: "The fact that gossip had published the banns was one of the reasons I had come

East. You can't stop going with an old friend on account of rumours, and on the other hand I had no intention of being rumoured into marriage.'' When he begins to think himself in love with Jordan, Nick remembers the girl at home:

> I am slow-thinking and full of interior rules that act as brakes on my desires, and I knew that first I had to get myself definitely out of that tangle back home. I'd been writing letters once a week and signing them: "Love, Nick," and all I could think of was how, when that certain girl played tennis, a faint moustache of perspiration appeared on her upper lip. Nevertheless there was a vague understanding that had to be tactfully broken off before I was free.

Nick is indeed full of interior rules; it is a condition of his honesty. But it is also a condition of his coldness. He is so reserved, such a careful scrutineer of persons, their dispositions and their motives, that he is near incapable of achieving any close relationship. Nick's account of his affair with a girl in New York confirms this. He treats her in much the same way, and for the same reasons, as the girl at home: "I even had a short affair with a girl who lived in Jersey City and worked in the accounting department, but her brother began throwing mean looks in my direction, so when she went on her vacation in July I let it blow quietly away." In both cases, Nick abandons the relationship in order that his intentions may not be misinterpreted by third persons. He is more anxious that his honesty be publicly recognized, than he is to achieve any genuine intimate relationship.

It is fitting that Nick should toy with the idea of loving Jordan, whom he admires for her self-sufficiency. As Gatsby projects his romantic heroic dreams onto Daisy, so Nick projects his sceptical anti-heroic vision onto Jordan. Both girls become symbolic of their admirers' fantasies; both seem to promise the state of being each eagerly seeks. But where Daisy fails Gatsby by not measuring up to his vision, Jordan educates Nick by showing him the inadequacy of his.

Nick's rupture with Jordan shows him that honesty is not a simple value, that cleanness and simplicity are not enough in the conduct of personal relations. It marks, moreover, the beginning of Nick's maturity. The initial break occurs during a telephone conversation, shortly after Myrtle Wilson's death. "We talked like that for a while," says Nick, "and then abruptly we weren't talking any longer. I don't know which of us hung up with a sharp click, but I know I didn't care." Nick is puzzled by this departure from his own normal routine, and seeks to tidy things up in a final meeting: "I wanted to leave things in order and not just trust that obliging and indifferent sea to sweep my refuse away." But this final meeting forces Nick to recognize the complexity of human beings and their relations. Jordan rebukes him for his attitude: "I thought you were rather an honest and straightforward person. I thought it was your secret pride." Nick however is no longer so assured about the nature of honesty. "I'm thirty," he says, "I'm five years too old to lie to myself and call it honour." Nick has in fact discovered human complexity within himself: "She didn't answer. Angry, and half in love with her, and tremendously sorry, I turned away."

On reflection, Nick learns, not merely to assess experience honestly, but to accept the paradoxes of human conduct and personality, with sympathy as well as understanding. He learns to look at life through a variety of windows, from more than one point of view, and to accept the sobering wisdom this achievement brings. As he says on a more trivial occasion, "It is invariably saddening to look through new eyes at things upon which you have expended your own powers of adjustment."

The different ways in which Gatsby and Nick contrast sharpen the difference between the two sorts of hero, and this is nowhere more evident than in their attitudes to time. To the hero of romance, time is insignificant. In the Arthurian romances characters exist in a timeless world; no one ages or dies of natural causes; questing after the Sangreal, the hero seeks a timeless truth. The great age of the Round Table, in the *Morte d'Arthur*, passes away not naturally, but through treachery and catastrophe. "Childe Roland to the Dark Tower Came" is a poem intensely aware of its era, of the mid-nineteenth century, its peculiar problems and anxieties; but it is a poem, nevertheless, in the romance tradition. Despite "the woe of years," the Childe is able to confront his timeless destiny. The normal processes of time even seem to be waived so that he may recognize the Tower:

> Not see? because of night perhaps?—Why, day
> Came back again for that! before it left,
> The dying sunset kindled through a cleft.
>> (st. xxxii)

The hero of the novel of sentimental education, on the other hand, exists very much in time, and changes with time. David Copperfield and Clarissa discover truth only in time, and are altered through and by time. The consciousness of each is shaped by time.

The Great Gatsby is a novel deeply concerned with time. It contains repeated allusions to hours, days and seasons suggestive of change. At the beginning of the novel, Nick has "that familiar conviction that life was beginning again with summer." In chapter 5 he speaks of the end of the afternoon, "the hour of profound human change"; in chapter 6 of "a cool night with that mysterious excitement in it which comes at the two changes of the year." Jordan says, in chapter 7, "Life starts all over again when it gets crisp in the fall"; and Nick meditates on his age: "I was thirty. Before me stretched the portentous, menacing road of a new decade." On the morning after Mrs. Wilson's death, Nick notices "an autumn flavour in the air," and at the end of the novel he says, "when the blue smoke of brittle leaves was in the air and the wind blew the wet laundry stiff on the line I decided to come back home."

Most of these observations on time and change are made by Nick in his role as narrator. He has learned to respect time. But during the course of the events he describes in the novel, he was tempted to forget it:

> Thirty—the promise of a decade of loneliness, a thinning list of single men to know, a thinning brief-case of enthusiasm, thinning hair. But there was Jordan beside me, who, unlike Daisy, was too wise ever to carry well-forgotten dreams from age to age. As we passed over the dark bridge her wan face fell lazily against my coat's shoulder and the formidable stroke of thirty died away with the reassuring pressure of her hand.

Gatsby, on the other hand, as befits a hero of romance, never once deigns to recognize time. He is prepared to wait years for Daisy, and to unlearn those intervening years when he thinks at last he has her. Nick warns him that Daisy might not be capable of this:

> "I wouldn't ask too much of her," I ventured. "You can't repeat the past."
> "Can't repeat the past?" he cried incredulously. "Why of course you can!"
> He looked around him wildly, as if the past were lurking here in the shadow of his house, just out of reach of his hand.
> "I'm going to fix everything just the way it was before," he said, nodding determinedly. "She'll see."

But Gatsby fails to abolish the past for Daisy. She is unable to say she never loved Tom.

Nick, however, learns the importance of time, the way time modifies value. He learns that human experience must be understood in the context of time, human affairs adjusted to a recognition of time. He learns ultimately the generosity that follows when we see each other moving through time towards death:

> Gatsby believed in the green light, the orgastic future that year by year recedes before us. It eluded us then, but that's no matter—to-morrow we

will run faster, stretch out our arms still further . . . And one fine morning—
    So we beat on, boats against the current, borne back ceaselessly into
the past.

Another difference between the two sorts of hero is in what they
recognize as real. Nick and Gatsby see different realities. Gatsby's is
naturally that of the hero of romance. The everyday is unreal for him;
reality is what he has discovered through his dreams. The hero of the
novel of sentimental education lives in a world where reality is elusive:
he thinks he possesses it, but finally discovers it only when his education
is completed. The hero of romance, on the other hand, is from the beginning acquainted with reality, though he may have to wait to possess
it, as Childe Roland has to wait for the Dark Tower. Heredity makes
Gatsby a dreamer. His father, whom we meet only after the son's death,
like Gatsby prefers the image to the object. He sets more value on an old
and cherished photograph of Gatsby's mansion than on the mansion itself.
"He had shown it so often," remarks Nick, "that I think it was more
real to him now than the house itself." There is irony in Gatsby's dying
at the hand of just such another dreamer, Wilson who projects a dream
of divine providence onto the massive eyes of Doctor T. J. Eckleburg
watching over the valley of ashes.
    Gatsby's apprehension of reality is explained in a much quoted
passage:

> The truth was that Jay Gatsby of West Egg, Long Island, sprang from his
> Platonic conception of himself. He was a son of God—a phrase which, if
> it means anything, means just that—and he must be about His Father's
> business, the service of a vast, vulgar, and meretricious beauty. So he
> invented just the sort of Jay Gatsby that a seventeen-year-old boy would
> be likely to invent, and to this conception he was faithful to the end.

Gatsby touches all his surroundings with his gaudy idealism, in an effort
to persuade himself of the "unreality of reality." Owl-eyes, the sympathetic drunk inexplicably adrift in Gatsby's world, marvels that the books
in his library are real—not "nice durable cardboard"—and compares
Gatsby to Belasco, the producer noted for his insistence on authentic
properties. Like Belasco, Gatsby is more of a showman than an artist,
but he puts his heart into the show. Daisy could not but fall short of
Gatsby's dream, Nick points out: "It had gone beyond her, beyond everything. He had thrown himself into it with creative passion, adding to it
all the time, decking it out with every bright feather that drifted his way.
No amount of fire or freshness can challenge what a man can store up
in his ghostly heart."

Nick imagines Gatsby's disenchantment with Daisy and with his dream before he is murdered by Wilson:

> He must have looked up at an unfamiliar sky through frightening leaves and shivered as he found what a grotesque thing a rose is and how raw the sunlight was upon the scarcely created grass. A new world, material without being real, where poor ghosts, breathing dreams like air, drifted fortuitously about . . . like that ashen, fantastic figure gliding towards him through the amorphous trees.

Whether Gatsby at last abandoned his dream of reality or not, is less important than "the colossal vitality of his illusion," at its height. Even more important is what Nick learns about reality from contemplating Gatsby's illusion.

From the beginning of the events described in the novel, Nick observes his surroundings with candour and with imagination, but there is something lacking. His imagination is capable only of aesthetic excursions. Getting drunk in Tom and Myrtle's lofty love nest, he thinks how the windows of the apartment must appear to watchers in the streets:

> Yet high over the city our line of yellow windows must have contributed their share of human secrecy to the casual watcher in the dark streets, and I saw him too, looking up and wondering. I was within and without, simultaneously enchanted and repelled by the inexhaustible variety of life.

Nick's sensitivity to the complexities and subtleties of aesthetic apprehension contrasts with the insensitivity of Mr. McKee, the photographer, whose portfolio contains studies with titles like "Beauty and the Beast . . . Loneliness . . . Old Grocery Horse . . . Brook'n Bridge . . ." It is this sensitivity that Nick shows in his response to Gatsby, Gatsby's parties, Gatsby's possessions; he refrains from oversimplifying, neither sparing the absurdity, nor ignoring the glamour.

But it takes time for Nick to reach the point where he can extend this sensitivity from aesthetic into moral judgment. He does not believe all the scandal about Gatsby, but he disapproves of him, and for the greater part of the novel keeps him at a distance, as it were, by treating him purely as an aesthetic phenomenon. Gatsby's extraordinary account of his life provokes only delighted irony from Nick: "Then it was all true. I saw the skins of tigers flaming in his palace on the Grand Canal: I saw him opening chests of rubies to ease, with their crimson-lighted depths, the gnawings of his broken heart." Only slowly, and in spite of himself, does Nick come to appreciate the human and moral reality of Gatsby, to appreciate that "the inexhaustible variety of life" is operative at the moral as well as at the aesthetic level.

Towards the end of the novel, Nick finds himself able, despite his moral training, to appreciate Gatsby as a man, to compliment him, "who represented everything for which I have an unaffected scorn," and to recognize his superiority to the Buchanans' set:

> "They're a rotten crowd," I shouted across the lawn. "You're worth the whole damn bunch put together."
>
> I've always been glad I said that. It was the only compliment I ever gave him, because I disapproved of him from beginning to end.

After Gatsby's death Nick realizes that he has entered—if only posthumously—into a substantial relationship with Gatsby: "it grew on me that I was responsible, because no one else was interested—interested, I mean, with that intense personal interest to which everyone has some vague right at the end." "We were close friends," he tells Gatsby's father. Nick will go back West, at first wanting no more "privileged glimpses into the human heart," but ready on reflection to accept the enlargement of his sympathies his experiences have produced.

The greatness of *The Great Gatsby*, it seems to me, lies primarily in the way it manages to catch the moment of change, in the development of the Western sensibility, when new attitudes to the heroic were taking shape. Nick is the hero with whom the reader, despite reservations, substantially identifies himself. Gatsby is too absurd, too astonishing. Yet Nick's sentimental education is overshadowed by Gatsby's dazzling career. We may identify with Nick, but our interest is focussed on Gatsby. The off-centre focus, it seems to me, dramatically represents the new configuration of attitudes towards the heroic. Before 1914, let us say, writers were able, either to believe in the possibilities of romantic heroism, like Browning, or to burlesque it, like Jane Austen, pointing to the more appropriate heroism of self-discovery. But even for Jane Austen, heroic action in the world at large is possible. Young officers can win fame, fortune and honour at sea.

What is new about *The Great Gatsby* is that, at the same time, it points to the necessity for heroic effort in self-discovery, burlesques romantic heroism, and laments its passing. This is perhaps where the novel is truly American. It is peculiarly the American experience to witness the disappearance of opportunities for heroic action in the world at large. But it is the experience of all Western nations too. Americans have only felt it more vividly. Philip Rahv complains of "the dissociation of mind from experience" in American literature, as if it were the fault of American writers, but this dissociation, surely, is a result of the events of modern history, the conditions of modern social life in all developed nations.

The Great Gatsby, then, is a novel about this very dissociation, and a pre-eminently successful one because it evokes the experience of dissociation in vividly human terms. Nick, busy with self-discovery, is nevertheless fascinated by the spectacle of Gatsby attempting heroic action and heroic devotion old-style, and his sentimental education is incomplete until he is able to recognize and accept the thwarted and perverted impulses on which Gatsby's efforts are based, until he is able to feel the loss so eloquently expressed in his threnody for experiences of the sort enjoyed by the discoverers of Long Island:

> Gradually I became aware of the old island here that flowered once for Dutch sailors' eyes—a fresh, green breast of the new world. Its vanished trees, the trees that had made way for Gatsby's house, had once pandered in whispers to the last and greatest of all human dreams; for a transitory enchanted moment man must have held his breath in the presence of this continent, compelled into an aesthetic contemplation he neither understood nor desired, face to face for the last time in history with something commensurate to his capacity for wonder.

Gatsby and the Failure of the Omniscient "I"

Ron Neuhaus

Fitzgerald himself was keenly aware that *Gatsby* was a flawed work, but the nature and origin of its major flaws escaped him. In a frank letter to Edmund Wilson in 1925, he explained what he takes to be the novel's "BIG FAULT."

> I gave no account of (and had no feeling about or knowledge of) the emotional relationship between Gatsby and Daisy from the time of their reunion to the catastrophe.

But his inability to handle relations between Gatsby and Daisy is merely symptomatic of more crucial faults in the novel: that of a breakdown in narrative technique, and an inability to create fully fleshed characters beneath the "blankets of excellent prose" Fitzgerald refers to later in the letter. *Gatsby* begins with first person narration, but Fitzgerald will not accept the limitation of this self-imposed restriction and constantly strains toward an "omniscient *I*" through diction, flashback, and reconstructed events. Despite his ingenuity, he fails to create a responsible fiction. He finds the first person perspective inadequate for the credibility of his moral stance, yet he will not take the responsibility involved with an omniscient perspective. The first person limitation enables him to avoid the scenes (as he notes in his letter) that his insights could not handle. Nick literally chaperones what could be scenes of revealing intimacy between Gatsby and Daisy.

Another factor, not stylistic but of strong influence, was the cultural climate of the post-war decade. The problems of character and style reflect

---

From *The Denver Quarterly* 12, no. 1 (Spring 1977). Copyright © 1977 by The University of Denver.

a mood in which a desire for moral security remained ("the world to be in uniform and at a sort of moral attention," as Nick says), but found itself in a world which could not provide that fulfillment. The moral authority of first person narrative was not adequate for such a context, and Fitzgerald tried to create esthetically what could not be discovered naturally. To this end, he experimented with multiple perspective. The efforts at extending perspective are admirable enough: the later movement into Gatsby's and Daisy's minds, into Michaelis' account of the car accident, as well as the intimate details of Gatsby's past—but through the early extended use of first person Fitzgerald has painted himself into a corner. As point of view makes some blatant shifts late in the novel, there is no sense of multiple perspective or modulation, but rather of an attempt to maintain, however thinly, the moral perspective of the first person narration, while at the same time trying to bring in third person credibility. The reader has a collection of fragments, conceivably from different perspectives, but what differentiates Fitzgerald from Pound, Eliot, Joyce, or Faulkner in his later work is that they did not structure their respective works around a solitary informing consciousness.

Conrad's *Heart of Darkness* furnishes a good model for the type of problem in *Gatsby*, as does Ford's *The Good Soldier*. But Marlow doesn't come across as an obtrusive sensibility, while Nick does. By the same token, Dowell's moral tone does not pretend to accurately assess the situation, but rather to characterize *him*. The genitive fault of *Gatsby* is not in the omission of certain scenes, but in Nick as a narrative voice. He lacks Marlow's effective transparency, and when the third person passages late in the book use the same rhetoric as Nick has used in his own voice, the congruity of tone makes us realize that there is in fact no ironic tone.

Were it not for this later under-cutting of irony, the opening paragraphs would provide a revealing anatomy of Nick through his commentary on the supposed moral climate in which he finds himself. In the full run of the book they provide an introduction to the sensibility of what will become the omniscient *I*. The first sentence sets the mood. "In my younger and more vulnerable years, my father gave me some advice that I've been turning over in my mind ever since." The crucial phrase here is "more vulnerable." It indicates that, in the scheme of things as perceived by the narrator, he occupies a position of some emotional and moral security, almost to the point of smugness. Fitzgerald does not dwell on this note, but shifts the focus to the nature of the advice, advice which predicates the existence of hereditary moral decency and, naturally, moral aristocracy. The tone is set for the third paragraph, in which Nick demonstrates a short-sightedness which his later explanations cannot offset. He points out that he is inclined to reserve all judgments, yet pontificates on psychology in the next sentence. "The abnormal mind is quick to detect and attach itself to this quality when it appears in a normal person . . ." As the sentence continues it reveals a sensibility that increasingly distances itself from literal reality by inflated rhetoric.

> . . . and so it came about that in college I was unjustly accused of being a politician, because I was privy to the secret grief of wild, unknown men.

This is virtually unintelligible. The diction evades understanding: "secret griefs," "wild, unknown men." The attention falls of necessity on the man using such diction to communicate his experience, such as it may be. The smugness becomes an almost leaden irony. Nick is not simply told things; on the contrary, he is "privy" to them. Later, in speaking of his war years, the diction shows his irony at its most arch. He does not just go into the army or off to war; rather he ". . . participated in that delayed Teutonic migration known as the Great War."

An inescapable problem with such a distancing tone is credibility. If, as a matter of course, the informing sensibility transforms reality into the adornments the mind projects, how can its evaluation be seen as authentic? its reconstruction of past events credible? its judgments appropriate? Fitzgerald's treatment of Nick establishes him as a character who cannot deal with the literal, and who must always construct an elaborate and moralistic rhetoric to insulate him from confrontation. Almost immediately, his smugness and complacency become too fulsome.

> The intimate revelations of young men, or at least, the terms in which they express them, are usually plagiaristic and marred by obvious suppressions.

Plagiaristic terms could well apply to the way in which Nick sees Gatsby later in the novel, yet he will not apply this observation to himself when he sees Gatsby in the borrowed phrase a "son of God," nor will he apply it to the plagiarized romanticizings of Gatsby.

Nick's limitations as an objective commentator are definitely established through the impressive architecture of one sequence in particular. Note the degree of smugness (or the injection of the author's rhetorical flourishes): ". . . as my father snobbishly suggested, and I snobbishly repeat, a sense of the fundamental decencies is parcelled out unequally at birth." The sentence is relentless in its assumption of a moral determinism as absolute as that of Calvin. It indicates a universe in which the snobbish Nick finds himself not only well placed, but one of the elect, possessed of congenital moral wealth. When he exercises his moral faculty, the prose approaches the gothic.

> It is what preyed on Gatsby, what foul dust floated in the wake of his dreams that temporarily closed out my interest in the abortive sorrows and short-winded elations of men.

Even if justified as a chracterization of the narrator, this is extreme. It no longer reveals, but cloys. However, a certain pattern of interpretation has been established in which the narrator infuses events with a diction that basically ignores their literal significance ("wild, unknown men" instead of "college freshmen"). As the novel progresses this pattern becomes embodied in images, events, and actions. Any banal event, any simple action will have embellishments heaped on it to create magnitude and significance.

As one check on this, whatever Nick or the omniscient voice in the later part of the book tells us about Gatsby, we must keep in mind the literal man (such aspects as are given) and his goal. Gatsby is a man trying to break up a marriage in order that he may resume a relationship with a woman who is bland at her most appealing. Concerning the man himself, although we are told that "Gatsby turned out all right," we must remember that he was a passenger witness to a hit-and-run homicide, and was not fluffed in the least by it. His criminal contacts do not bother him, and he has an almost total insensitivity to human nature.

Yet, given the assumptions of Nick's rhetoric (and ultimately, Fitzgerald's), anything can be transformed into anything else, including its literal opposite. Given this, whatever is most characterless, banal, or undefined can be more easily assigned qualities, since it has no strong features of its own, and can so allow the projecting consciousness fuller play. It may even follow that this type of sensibility will seek out the vague and shallow elements of life in order to exercise this faculty. An early metaphor for just this process occurs in the "valley of ashes" trope which introduces chapter 2. The literal image is that of a dumping ground with drifting dust clouds. But under the transformative vision of Nick (in a third person tone), the literal scene functions as a blank screen on which forms are first projected, and then assumed to be innate.

> This is a valley of ashes—a fantastic farm where ashes grow like wheat ... where ashes take on the form of houses and chimneys ... of ash-gray men who move dimly and already crumbling through the powdery air.

The literal aspect is clear: here is a locale of shifting dust where ashes and clouds of dust can be imagined to take on forms. But the prose quickly abandons the metaphorical origin of the forms, and the illusion receives treatment as though it were a literal event.

> Occasionally a line of gray cars crawls along an invisible track, gives out a ghastly creak, and comes to rest, and immediately the ash-gray men swarm up with leaden spades and stir up an impenetrable cloud, which screens their obscure operations from your sight.

The description is very deft, and must be reread for assurance that this is in fact an evolved illusion, not a real scene. The illusion grows out of a literal vagueness, presents itself as a definite scene, and then dissolves into a vagueness generated by that scene. It reveals the informing sensibility of the novel (which is not Nick Carraway's) at work on a landscape. The same technique of disguising reality obtains in Gatsby's idealization of Daisy and his romance with her, of Tom's attraction to racism (especially his observation that it was all "scientific stuff"), and of Nick's creation of Gatsby's identity.

The "valley of ashes" trope parallels in method the rhetoric at the eginning of chapter 1. There, too, Fitzgerald used an inflated rhetoric, the "abortive sorrows," the "riotous excursions . . . into the human heart." Here, the process develops into a series of images imposed upon the formless. It moves from the literal "desolate area" to the figurative "valley of ashes" to the metaphorical "ashes grow like wheat" to the mimetic "ashes take the form of houses . . . of ash-gray men" to the actual, the "gray cars" passage above. In the final stage, the transformative process has been forgotten, and the illusion becomes the reality.

Following this, we see the enormous eyes of Dr. T. J. Eckleburg, an image of sterile vision, vision that has no connection with any past, or any particular origin. The oculist's sign could be seen as a symbol of an omniscient God, but not in this novel. The context of images, as well as the narrative voice, deals with the human problem of perception and interpretation, and of the subsequent verbal units used to evade the literal world by the "westerners," and to a much lesser degree by the party goers who playfully ascribe mysterious and shady histories to Gatsby. Had the narrative voice remained within focus, the novel could have been a superb exploration of the ironies in attempting to discover values and grand identities in a world which does not contain them. In such a world, in order to find gold one must seed the mine, and then forget the deception.

This ironic technique can work well as a structuring device, an informing metaphor, and also provide a core around which to build a character, all of which effects occur in the first half of *Gatsby*. But when Fitzgerald tries to use it as a means to move into a third person point of view, and have this baroque subjectivity function with the authority of an omniscient voice, the narrative structure of the book begins to crumble. One excellent example of this comes immediately before Gatsby is shot, at the end of chapter 8. As far as Nick knows, Gatsby has merely been waiting for a call from Daisy. But Nick moves from this to an amplification and speculation on the event, and then, as in the ashes trope, reaches a certainty. In his initiating speculation, he begins conservatively, with a straightforward qualification. "I have an idea that Gatsby himself didn't believe it would come, and perhaps he no longer cared." This pretends to be nothing more than honest speculation. Yet he immediately jumps from this to an elaborate hypothesis which assumes the tone of verity. "If that was true he must have felt that he had lost the old warm world, paid a high price for living too long with a single dream." At this point, we have definitely lost touch with Gatsby's consciousness. Losing the "old warm world" is not in his diction. Fitzgerald labors it even further, as the narrative voice fully enters the world of its own speculations, and responds to them with its own sensibility.

> He must have looked up at an unfamiliar sky through frightening leaves and shivered as he found what a grotesque thing a rose is and how raw the sunlight was upon the scarcely created grass.

This is impossible to read as an insight into Gatsby's character; it becomes a blanket, not a window. Yet if we read it only adding to Nick's character, it repeats what we already know. But Fitzgerald is trying awkwardly to reach toward an "omniscient *I*" and we lose both Gatsby and Nick in the process. The tone also gives an intimation that Nick has never been ours at all; we have had only a mask and a device to conceal a lack of character development. The passage concludes with an ooze of saccharine rhetoric addressed to no one, from no one, and about no one whose identity has been established in the fiction.

> A new world, material without being real, where poor ghosts, breathing dreams like air, drifted fortuitously about . . . like that ashen, fantastic figure gliding toward him through the amorphous trees.

We are asked to see the judgments of a narrative voice, not as that of a particular character who forces his interpretation onto a reality incompatible with them, but that of a trustworthy narrator, almost an omniscient voice presenting us with legitimate insights into the world of the fiction.

Still, we may be, by some stretch of perspective, within Nick's consciousness. But earlier, at the end of chapter 6, we have a passage whose details would be totally inaccessible to Nick, yet the diction and tone belong to what we expect to be his voice. At this point we can no longer withhold the observation that the stylistic aberrations which could have been seen as character development of the narrator must now be laid to the author as flaws in the narrative structure. In the following passage, through the third person perspective, we are totally in Gatsby's mind; Nick is nowhere near as a justified mediator, and we have no idea where this information comes from.

> Out of the corner of his eye Gatsby saw that the blocks of the sidewalks really formed a ladder and mounted to a secret place above the trees—he could climb to it, if he climbed alone, and once there he could suck on the pap of life, gulp down the incomparable milk of wonder.

At the end of the chapter the prose goes even further afield, and confirms that much of what had earlier passed for ironic language was, in actuality, maudlin sincerity. The irony of the novel has been totally undercut. For Nick to take his own romanticizing insights seriously might reveal his character; for Fitzgerald to present the diction of these insights as informative comment indicates a great flaw in his creation.

> He knew that when he kissed this girl, and forever wed his unutterable visions to her perishable breath, his mind would never romp again like the mind of God. . . . At his lips' touch she blossomed for him like a flower and the incarnation was complete.

Fitzgerald wants to deal with superhuman characters, people whose thoughts might plausibly romp like God's, but he can't create them; he can only raise the type of prose associated with them. Nineteen twenty-five was too late for such characters to be treated sincerely, and yet Fitzgerald doesn't want to maintain the mask of irony. He wants us to somehow take the story of Gatsby seriously—otherwise we would always have the buffer of Nick as an ironist. To this end, the passage above employs the tactics of smooth propaganda: the glittering phrase, the slick allusion, the "deep" thought. The technique can be pleasing, well-cadenced, and with great surface attraction. But it can not be responsible fiction, no matter how adept its rhetoric. We have too many Gatsbys, and not only are they unrelated but they are not rooted in the text. If, as Nick speculates at the beginning of the novel, "personality is an unbroken series of successful gestures," Gatsby as a character has no personality. His development is, at best, a broken series of unsuccessful gestures. There is nothing to connect the implied heroism of "unutterable visions" or "son of God" with the Gatsby we see; nothing to connect the "old sport" Gatsby with the romantic figure of Nick's narration. Even so, Fitzgerald makes the most extreme attributions to Gatsby in the omniscient voice, and these ignore the literal man as he has been portrayed in the same manner that Nick ignores the basic quality of the reality around him. What is haunting about Gatsby, if anything, is not his "extraordinary gift for hope," but that he is actually so banal.

The failure in voice leads to other weaknesses in the narration. Not only does Fitzgerald have difficulty in rendering his evaluations of Gatsby, he has great difficulty in setting up the machinery to bring in particular material about him to occasion the romanticizing prose. One notable case is in the sequence after the auto accident, when Nick says that Gatsby tells him the story of his youth. Up to this point Gatsby has not been particularly open with Nick, nor has he indicated a desire to be. But Fitzgerald wants to play around with Gatsby's past, and tries to account for his motivation by using a poetic metaphor to distract the reader from the improbability of the confession. According to Nick, Gatsby ". . . told it to me because 'Jay Gatsby' had broken up like glass against Tom's hard malice. . . ." The metaphor is interesting, but it doesn't cover the fact that Fitzgerald has failed to provide a fictive motivation for the confession. He could have solved the problem by using third person, but he has to maintain the limited point of view as a vehicle for value judgments and highly extravagant diction. Also, he has failed to create a character with sufficient substance to supply an omniscient perspective with material. The mask of first person narration protects him to a degree, but ultimately it fails to conceal the fact that the "BIG FAULT" was not that he had no notion of the "relations" between Gatsby and Daisy, but that he had developed no characters of sufficient depth to have relations.

Chapter 8, more than any other, dodges from one perspective to another in an effort to substitute expanse for depth. We are in Nick's mind, Gatsby's mind, even Daisy's mind. One interesting passage gives an excerpt from Gatsby's talk with Nick and thus provides a measure for what is attributed to him earlier and later. His own diction is direct, unembellished, and with a functional banality that allows Nick (Fitzgerald's omniscient voice at this point) to project on to it whatever he chooses.

> "I can't describe to you how surprised I was to find out I loved her, old sport. . . . Well, there I was, 'way off my ambitions, getting deeper in love every minute, and all of a sudden I didn't care. What was the use of doing great things if I could have a better time telling her what I was going to do?"

Compare this with the supposed reconstruction of a past event that follows. Is it likely that Gatsby would recount to Nick the details of his intimacy with Daisy? and with such attention to particulars?

> It was a cold fall day, with a fire in the room and her cheeks flushed. Now and then she moved and he changed his arm a little, and once he kissed her dark shining hair. . . . They had never been closer in their month of love, nor communicated more profoundly one with another. . . .

Only if we could imagine Gatsby saying to Nick, "Once I kissed her dark shining hair, old sport, and we never communicated more profoundly with one another than then," would the passage be acceptable. But at this point clearly there are two novels being written here: one from Nick's ironic perspective, and one from third person. Yet they share the same voice. One paragraph later, when we see things from Daisy's perspective, any pretense of this being a narrative from Nick's point of view has vanished—with absolutely no fictive modulation. The material is simply unloaded onto the page.

> Through this twilight universe Daisy began to move again with the season; suddenly she was again keeping half a dozen dates with half a dozen men, and drowsing asleep at dawn with the beads and chiffon of an evening dress tangled among dying orchids on the floor beside her bed. And all the time something within her was crying for a decision.

The nature of the difficulty here can be brought out by a question: if Fitzgerald can move into omniscient author here, why can't he use it in the crucial scenes between Gatsby and Daisy? When Gatsby takes Daisy through his house, Nick comes along as a chaperone at their request. Gatsby particularly wants him there, and when Nick tries to go Fitzgerald attempts a weak justification for keeping him there. "I tried to go then, but they wouldn't hear of it; perhaps my presence made them feel more satisfactorily alone." Conceivably, the lovers might feel reluctant to enter into an intimacy which being alone might force, but the problem here is that of style and character, not of thought. Fitzgerald has created such literally vapid and unfilled-out lovers that the love story can only be maintained by keeping them out of the reader's sight, and by attributive rhetoric to supply what characterization does not. Given what he has created (or failed to create), he can't bring them together, because they lack sufficient depth to work in a love scene. His switches in perspective attempt to draw the reader's attention away from this, much as a series of clever camera shots can distract a viewer from the superficiality of a movie love scene. Fitzgerald predicates an ideal, but his prose cannot work up to it. He is unable at this point in his career to provide characters as suitable vehicles for insight. Having created mere outlines, he can only adorn, not reveal.

Had Fitzgerald not used third person as a platform for his romanticizing, his efforts to work toward a type of omniscient quality would have made a more substantial novel. Some of the approaches to a third person perspective are quite ingenious, as when Nick describes a typical Gatsby party. The information in the description is far beyond what he would have access to, but the passage is smoothly done. We begin with emblematic detail and end up with the flushed jaundice of expressionistic rhetoric.

> By seven o'clock the orchestra has arrived, no thin five-piece affair, but a whole pitful of oboes and trombones . . .

> The lights grow brighter as the earth lurches away from the sun, and now the orchestra is playing yellow cocktail music. . . .

Fitzgerald handles it differently when he uses the ploy of a timetable dated July 5 on which Nick writes down the "names of those who came to Gatsby's house that summer." The mention of the day following Independence Day is intriguing, as is the image of society being numbered on a timetable. But it is unlikely that Nick, as a character, would gather such information as "All these people," and the parties themselves do not maintain a custom of name giving. The catalogue is an early effort at an "omniscient *I*," but does not obtrude as much as the later shifts in perspective. However, the smoothest attempt comes with the diary brought by Gatsby's father. The incident has some credibility, and provides a different perspective within the limits of the first person narrative.

But on the whole the shifts in perspective destroy any integrity in the fiction. Yet Fitzgerald's failure of narrative voice in *Gatsby* comes in part because he is trying to make first person narrative do something which, by 1925, could no longer be done. He wants us to look at a highly romanticized (not merely romantic) figure and grant it serious consideration, to trust the teller and not the tale. The ideal and the characters he postulates do not fit the reality in which he wants them to exist, a reality roughly parallel to his own social and historical context, and his evasions take the form of switches and dodges in point of view in order to conceal the basic shallowness of his vision. He can handle only the plot of the romance; he cannot create the people necessary to animate it. For all that Gatsby tells Nick, never does he refer to any recent contact with Daisy—a void in the narration which corresponds to that of figures seen in shadow profile. Ironically, the firmest character in the book is the distinctly unromantic Meyer Wolfsheim.

In *Lord Jim* and *Heart of Darkness* Conrad handled the problem of the "omnisicient *I*" much better than did Fitzgerald, perhaps because he was not as anxious about getting credence for an unrealistic romanticization and its corresponding philosophy. But Fitzgerald has an afflicting ambivalence; he sensed that the somber moralizing of Nick could not be anything but ironic in modern fiction, yet he yearned for a modern context to validate a romanticizing moral sensibility. His problems with style and point of view begin as soon as he tries to present an unrealized character in sympathetic and favorable light. Fitzgerald refuses to be confined within first person, yet he will not accept the responsibility of omniscient author, because he cannot develop characters adequate to his vision of what those characters should be. Gatsby is a figment of the imagination of the novel that bears his name. For this reason, there are no "emotional relations" accounted for between him and Daisy.

The failings in *The Great Gatsby* are fascinating, and it survives as a novel quite possibly because of the intriguing nature of its weaknesses. We reject Carraway's pompous moralizing after the first few paragraphs, and his reliability as a witness by the end of the second chapter; yet when his voice occurs later under the aegis of third person, trying to construct insights and gain sympathy for Gatsby, we cannot help but reject it there as well. Yet the later use calls upon us to reject, not the credibility of a narrator, but that of the author.

Another Reading of *The Great Gatsby*

Keath Fraser

*Begin with an individual, and before you know it you find that you
have created a type; begin with a type, and you find that you have
created—nothing. That is because we are all queer fish, queerer behind
our faces and voices than we want any one to know or than we know
ourselves. When I hear a man proclaiming himself an "average, honest,
open fellow," I feel pretty sure that he has some definite and perhaps
terrible abnormality which he has agreed to conceal—and his
protestation of being average and honest and open is his way of
reminding himself of his misprision.*
Narrator in "The Rich Boy"

*Every one suspects himself of at least one of the cardinal virtues, and
this is mine: I am one of the few honest people that I have ever known.*
Narrator in The Great Gatsby

"Gonnegtions" are of course important in *The Great Gatsby*, for without
them Gatsby's rumoured association with crime, and its particular dialect, would not ring as true. The presence of Wolfsheim serves to connect
Gatsby with the underworld from which his riches are hatched and his
plans to marry Daisy made possible. "Gonnegtions" are Gatsby's dream,
and also Nick's. What Gatsby of West Egg is seeking, by means of the
lucrative business afforded by the underworld portrayed in Wolfsheim,
is a con*egg*tion with Daisy Fay of East Egg. In this light, Gatsby's "Platonic conception of himself" is enriched by what I take to be Fitzgerald's
allusion to Plato's parable in *The Symposium* about the origin of love.
In *The Symposium* Aristophanes is made to tell how Zeus, angered at
the behaviour of the three circular shapes constituting the original sexes,
decides to cut each in half: like eggs, says Plato, sliced in half by a hair.
Yearning ever since to be reunited with himself, man has sought to couple
with his other half. According to Plato, the resultant halves of the original
hermaphrodite became heterosexual men and women; halves of the original female, lesbian, women; while fragments of the first male turned
into men who have devoted their lives (honourably in Plato's eyes) to
the intimacy of boys and other men ("it requires," says Plato, "the compulsion of convention to overcome their natural disinclination to marriage and procreation"). If *The Great Gatsby* is a love story, and it is, it
is one aware of this complex sexuality of antiquity. As we shall see, it
is not only to *The Symposium* that we must turn for confirmation of the

From *English Studies in Canada* 3 (Autumn 1979). Copyright ©1979 by the Association
of Canadian University Teachers of English.

novel's peculiar and hitherto unnoticed sexuality—the theme of what follows—but also to *The Satyricon* of Petronius.

Here and there in Fitzgerald's novel inklings of depravity turn reader into voyeur. One never quite knows, for example, how to read the last page of chapter 2, a scene which follows the dissolute party in Myrtle Wilson's apartment, when Nick Carraway follows Mr. McKee out to the elevator. Descending, McKee suggests Nick have lunch with him some day—anywhere—and the elevator boy snaps: "Keep your hands off the lever." Apologetic, McKee says he was unaware he was touching it. The narrator says he would be glad to go. Where they go is to McKee's bedroom: ". . . I was standing beside his bed and he was sitting up between the sheets, clad in his underwear, with a great portfolio in his hands." Then some more of the narrator's ellipses between what we presume are titles of photographs taken by McKee are followed by Nick's abrupt removal to "the cold lower level" of Pennsylvania Station where he lies waiting for the morning train. It is an odd scene because Nick never goes to lunch with McKee and McKee never reappears. Odder still is the fact that Nick joins McKee in his apartment when no invitation, apart from the one to lunch, is spoken, and no rapport between the two men at Myrtle's party is established—except for Nick's having wiped a spot of dried lather from McKee's cheekbone when McKee has dozed off in a chair.

What I am about to suggest is that the quality of concealment in *The Great Gatsby* is adroit enough to have caused us to read over scenes we are intended to read through. Is there in the novel a cultivated ambiguity, such as that of the McKee episode, which flirts with, but never answers the question of Nick Carraway's sexuality, because Nick refuses to tell us the whole truth about himself? What is recoverable of Fitzgerald's earliest intentions, in Bruccoli's edition of *The Great Gatsby: A Facsimile of the Manuscript* (1973), may help to cloud the issue more than clear it up. Deleted from the novel we now have are words, phrases, and sentences of a section which, in the manuscript, follows directly from what now is the conclusion of chapter 2—that is, the scene in McKee's bedroom. (In the final version of the novel this section, which concludes with the second epigraph quoted above, is removed to become the conclusion to chapter 3, the account of Gatsby's first party.) More willing in the *Facsimile*, it would seem, to acknowledge the ambiguous nature of the bedroom scene, Fitzgerald pauses to compound the mystery by conceding that "a false impression" has been given by virtue of the fact that the few events discussed thus far in the story appear to have occupied all of Nick's time. Fitzgerald's original intention, if it can be rescued from pencilled-out lines in the manuscript, was to suggest that these events, in Nick's words, "were merely incidents sandwiched in between other incidents that interested me or fascinated just as much—in fact the man I balled around with most all summer doesn't appear in this story at all." This revelation is cancelled out in favour of the more concealed phrase, "my own affairs"—which became the phrase we now have, "my personal affairs." It may be merely coincidental that McKee, who never reappears, and the man Nick says he "balled around with most"—but who is hushed up—appear at the same stage of the original novel, when Fitzgerald is in the process of establishing the character of his narrator. Yet sexual implications, even in the muted final version, are not lost on us, and in the manuscript do serve to challenge our accepted reading of Nick's sexuality.

In this section of the *Facsimile* Nick goes on to mention a brief affair with a girl from the accounting department of Probity Trust company he works for in New York. The reason for his letting "the affair blow quietly away," in the manuscript, is the same offered in the final version—because, according to Nick, the girl's brother "began throwing mean looks in my direction." What is perhaps revealing are Nick's original words, the words Fitzgerald began to use, then scratched out and buried beneath the curious reason Nick offers for his escape from this girl. The words he starts to use, to explain the breakup, are "but her brother began *favoring me with* . . ." (my emphasis). With what? It seems a peculiar phrase to start explaining the reason for leaving this brother's sister. Does the rewritten version lead us away from a more honest confession? Probity Trust—Nick's company—tends to affirm those qualities which Nick would have us believe are his—honesty, conscientiousness, uprightness—and yet one is left wondering whether Nick is telling us the whole truth about abandoning the girl, indeed the whole truth for abandoning any girl, especially the one out West. As for his dropping Jordan Baker, we have tended to believe him when he calls Jordan "incurably dishonest," and because of this seldom have we believed Jordan when she, in turn, claims Nick to have been less than honest and straightforward in his relationship with her.

In view of what has been presented so far it may not be too soon to suggest that what Nick might in part be concealing, even escaping from, is what the narrator of "The Rich Boy" (agreed to be among Fitzgerald's finest short stories, and written immediately after *The Great Gatsby*) calls "abnormality." Perhaps we have taken Nick too much at his word—without trying to read through such a scene as the one in McKee's bedroom with the whole of Nick's character in view. Conceivably, his penetrating self-analysis on the opening page of the novel has lulled us into accepting his own protestation of being "normal."

He appears to begin his story in a way calculated to disarm his reader, encouraging him "to reserve all judgments." By suggesting that he himself has refrained from criticizing others—by following his father's advice—Nick may be pleading his own case with us. "The abnormal mind," he observes, "is quick to detect and attach itself to this quality when it appears in a normal person, and so it came about that in college I was unjustly accused of being a politician, because I was privy to the secret griefs of wild, unknown men." Such men, alongside Nick, are categorized by him as "abnormal" because they are attracted to him. And so when "an intimate revelation was quivering on the horizon" he has tried to appear tolerant, yet disinterested: "for the intimate revelations of young men, or at least the terms in which they express them, are usually plagiaristic and marred by obvious suppressions." The choice of words and phrases is peculiar. Why, for example, are such intimate revelations—flawed as they are by plagiarism and suppression—"abnormal"? Presumably, because such revelations are offered by "unknown" men, and are therefore gauche and indiscreet. But rather than perceiving these as a "normal" hazard for a man as attractive to other men as Nick boasts he is, he condemns them as belonging to those who were born with rather less than their share of "the fundamental decencies." Mainly because of his disarming admission of snobbery, we have always been convinced of Nick's own fundamental decencies—indeed doubtful if there is another narrator in modern literature more trustworthy than he. Yet in *The Satyricon* there is a narrator who is almost certainly as much a model for Fitzgerald's character as Conrad's trusty and frequently mentioned Marlow, and to that narrator's indecencies we will return.

For the moment it is worth going back to the second chapter in order to make sure the sexual nuances I have touched upon are clear enough to support the implications already made about McKee, and to anticipate some observations about others, including Nick, which remain to be made. McKee is introduced by the narrator as "a pale, feminine man from the flat below." He is, he tells Nick, in the "artistic game." His wife (who does not, incidentally, leave the party with her husband) tells Nick that her husband has photographed her a hundred and twenty-seven times since they were married. Nick calls her "handsome, and horrible." A bit later Tom Buchanan is amused at McKee's interest in getting more work on Long Island, if he can "get the entry," and suggests with a laugh that McKee "do some studies" of Myrtle's husband Wilson. Later still Wilson and McKee are discussed by their respective wives, and while Mrs. McKee is relieved to have escaped marrying a "kike," Myrtle claims to have in fact married one: "I thought he knew something about breeding, but he wasn't fit to lick my shoe." The allusion to breeding appears to be about class, but the drift beneath seems sexual. The highly-sexed Myrtle is childless; and her husband's impotence, if that is the reason for her constant desire to escape him, seems suitably complemented by the wasteland of ashes in which he dwells. Also childless, so far as we know, is Mrs. McKee, whose husband's assiduous use of his camera lens since their wedding appears to suggest a clear substitute for sex with his wife. Just as cars are what stimulate Wilson, as we shall see, so photographs can be seen to preoccupy McKee—particularly in the bedroom, where he shows his "great" portfolio to Nick, with the same hands which apologetically grasped the elevator lever moments earlier. This last glimpse of McKee between the sheets, while not the end of phallic imagery, illustrates what is typical of Fitzgerald's treatment of sex in the novel, that is, its ambiguity. It remains to be explored just how far, and for what reason, this ambiguity is deliberately cultivated by the narrator himself.

Still of little interest to scholars is the way Fitzgerald handles sexuality in his writings. The truly great artists, according to Virginia Woolf, are androgynous in mind, and Leslie Fiedler, in passing, has noted this interesting quality in Fitzgerald (it is a quality Fiedler is reluctant to admire): "In Fitzgerald's world, the distinction between sexes is fluid and shifting, precisely because he has transposed the mythic roles and values of male and female, remaking Clarissa in Lovelace's image, Lovelace in Clarissa's. With no difficulty at all and only a minimum of rewriting, the boy Francis, who was to be a center of vision in *The World's Fair*, becomes the girl Rosemary as that proposed novel turned into *Tender is the Night*. Thematically, archetypally even such chief male protagonists as Gatsby and Dick Diver are females." Fitzgerald himself, of course, acknowledged that "I am half feminine—at least my mind is. . . . Even my feminine characters are feminine Scott Fitzgeralds." This last sentence could be put another way: his masculine characters are masculine Scott Fitzgeralds, which is to say they are no less feminine than his own "half feminine" mind. At the party in Myrtle Wilson's flat, for example, Nick, looking out the window, makes an admission which is generally read as a comment on the tension created by the technique which critics have admired in the novel: Fitzgerald's ability to observe as well as to participate. "I was within and without, simultaneously enchanted and repelled by the inexhaustible variety of life." It has never been read as a suggestion of the narrator's epicene nature.

Writing to Maxwell Perkins before the publication of his novel, Fitzgerald confessed that "it may hurt the book's popularity that it's a *man's book*." By this he meant that his best characters were men and that his women faded out of the novel. In the same letter Fitzgerald had to agree with his editor that until now he had not revealed enough about Gatsby—which would allow Gatsby, and not Tom Buchanan, to dominate his story. Throughout the novel Nick holds the masculine forms of Gatsby and Tom in sharp contrast. For him, Gatsby's form seems preferable to Tom's, yet it is Tom's masculinity which captures Nick's attention in so convincing a manner that critics of the novel, in identifying the grander theme of the American dream, have perceived in Tom the cruel and palpable foil to Gatsby's idealism and illusion. For Nick the "gorgeous" Gatsby fails to come "alive" until Jordan Baker explains to him that Gatsby's house was deliberately chosen by its owner to be across the bay from Daisy's own house in East Egg. Then, says Nick, "He came alive to me, delivered suddenly from the womb of his purposeless splendor." In contrast to the insuperably *physical* purpose in the novel of Tom Buchanan, Gatsby and his purpose seem clearly metaphysical, springing agilely from that "Platonic conception of himself." Imagery associated with Gatsby suggests solipsism, sexlessness. It is otherwise with Tom: "Not even the effeminate swank of his riding clothes," Nick observes, "could hide the enormous power of that body—he seemed to fill those glistening boots until he strained the top lacing, and you could see a great pack of muscle shifting when his shoulder moved under his thin coat. It was a body capable of enormous leverage—a cruel body."

Here is a body of rather more interest to Nick than the one he courts in Jordan Baker. In fact, it fascinates him. As the novel progresses Tom's body comes to represent, far more than Gatsby's corruption and criminal associates do, the threat and evil force of the book. "Making a short deft movement, Tom Buchanan broke her nose with his open hand." The nose, of course, is Myrtle's. Myrtle's husband, on the other hand, suffers Tom's cruelty in a more subtle and central way, reaching its culmination on the fatal day Nick lunches with the Buchanans. The day is blisteringly hot. On his way to lunch Nick comments to himself, "That any one should care in this heat whose flushed lips he kissed, whose head made damp the pajama pocket over his heart!" Upon entering Tom's house he records what he overhears: " 'The master's body!' roared the butler into the mouthpiece. 'I'm sorry, madame, but we can't furnish it—it's far too hot to touch this noon!' " Nick then adds: "What he really said was: 'Yes . . . Yes . . . I'll see.' " In fact the caller is Myrtle's husband, hard up for cash, hoping Tom will sell him the car on which Wilson hopes to make enough profit to take his wife away. What Nick purports to hear first is an illusion, yet it is an illusion artistically contrived to make the scene which follows between Tom and Wilson at the garage all the more adroit with respect to the underlying competition between the two rivals for

Myrtle Wilson's favours. More particularly, it causes us to examine Nick's own narration of the scene.

> "Let's have some gas!" cried Tom roughly. "What do you think we stopped for—to admire the view?"
>
> "I'm sick," said Wilson without moving. "Been sick all day."
>
> "What's the matter?"
>
> "I'm all run down."
>
> "Well, shall I help myself?" Tom demanded. "You sounded well enough on the phone."
>
> With an effort Wilson left the shade and support of the doorway and, breathing hard, unscrewed the cap of the tank. In the sunlight his face was green.
>
> "I didn't mean to interrupt your lunch," he said. "But I need money pretty bad, and I was wondering what you were going to do with your old car."
>
> "How do you like this one?" inquired Tom. "I bought it last week."
>
> "It's a nice yellow one," said Wilson, as he strained at the handle.
>
> "Like to buy it?"
>
> "Big chance," Wilson smiled faintly. "No, but I could make some money on the other."
>
> "What do you want money for, all of a sudden?"
>
> "I've been here too long. I want to get away. My wife and I want to go West."

I want to suggest that this scene, like the McKee scene, is easily passed over, and that the sexual undertow adrift in the particular images which link Wilson and Tom has been carefully set up by Fitzgerald to contrast the two male rivals. We recall that three chapters earlier Nick has admired the incomparable form of Gatsby's car—the one Tom now is driving—"swollen here and there," observes Nick, "in its monstrous length." In *The Great Gatsby* it is worth remembering that the car is a symbol of masculinity, and the women (Jordan and Daisy) who drive cars do so badly, upsetting, even killing people. In the same chapter that Nick draws our attention to Gatsby's proud possession, he also glimpses "Mrs. Wilson straining at the garage pump with panting vitality as we went by." The scene above, with Tom and Wilson, seems therefore suggestive in the images it chooses to repeat. There is the elongated car driven by the potent Tom; and in the pump yet another phallic image, at which Wilson strains with rather less vitality than his wife, who has thrown him over for Tom.

At this point the afternoon sun continues to play chimerically with Nick's perception—this time of Wilson: "The relentless beating heat was beginning to confuse me and I had a bad moment there before I realized that so far his suspicions hadn't alighted on Tom." What follows is a curious generalization by Nick "that there was no difference between men, in intelligence or race, so profound as the difference between the sick and the well." It is precisely this difference one feels tempted to rephrase (without necessarily replacing one chimera with another), in order to suggest that in sexual terms what Fitzgerald is implying is that there is no difference so great as the difference between the normal and the abnormal. For Nick goes on to equate Wilson's sickness with guilt— and the simile he uses to illustrate this guilt is, it will have to be agreed, ambivalent: "Wilson was so sick that he looked guilty, unforgivably guilty—as if he just got some poor girl with child."

For Wilson (about whom we recall his wife having earlier said he knows nothing about "breeding"), such a potent act might indeed be upsetting, indeed abnormal. (Our sense of Wilson's guilt is made the more ambivalent perhaps by our recollection of Tom's earlier joke that Wilson would make quite a suitable study for the effeminate photographer McKee—"*George B. Wilson at the Gasoline Pump*." Naturally what Wilson looks guilty about is having had to lock up his wife—upstairs in the garage. This act is the reality Nick cannot foresee in chapter 2, when he and Tom first visit the garage, and Nick observes only half correctly, "It had occurred to me that this shadow of a garage must be a blind, and that sumptuous and romantic apartments were concealed overhead." There Nick's perception is illusory, but such perception has continued to bear upon what is normal and abnormal. On the day Myrtle is to die, Nick has overheard Tom telling Gatsby, "I've heard of making a garage out of a stable . . . but I'm the first man who ever made a stable out of a garage." As a stud, Tom clearly has what Wilson does not, though he, as much as Wilson, has made a mess of his relationship with Myrtle. The curious conjunction of these two men is the inevitable result of Nick's apparently random association of garages, cars, pumps, and cameras; for in spite of the romantic ideals normally associated with Nick, the reality of sex through his eyes is both a shifty and a mechanical proposition.

After Myrtle's death it is the "enormous leverage" of Tom's body (earlier observed by Nick in the same, apparently irrelevant way as the "lever" in the elevator with McKee) which seems to pry its way into the garage where Wilson has begun to come apart, gripping the doorposts of his office. "His eyes would drop slowly from the swinging light to the laden table by the wall, and then jerk back to the light again, and he gave out incessantly his high, horrible call: 'Oh, my Ga-od! Oh, my Ga-od! Oh, Ga-od! Oh, my Ga-od!' " This orgastic call emitted in mechanical jerks, seems complemented in the next sentence by Tom when he lifts his head with a "jerk" (the word repeated). Tom proceeds to extricate himself from the death for which he is, in effect, responsible (though of course, ironically, it is his wife who has driven over Myrtle, in Gatsby's car), by seizing Wilson "firmly by the upper arms," telling him "with soothing gruffness" to pull himself together. The narrator tells us Tom keeps "his hands firm on Wilson's body," insisting to the investigating policeman that Wilson is a friend of his, and claiming that the car which "did it" was yellow; the colour of his car, he says, is blue. Then he picks up Wilson "like a doll," deposits him in a chair, and escapes with Nick in tow. Worth noting, I think, is that Tom has no more perceived his cruelty to Wilson than he has his cruelty to Daisy, when much earlier she accuses him of injuring her little finger: "You did it, Tom . . . I know you didn't mean to, but you *did* do it. That's what I get for marrying a brute of a man, a great, big hulking physical specimen of a———" If it is the lover which intrigues Nick in Gatsby, it is the *man* which intrigues him in Tom; our failure to notice the delicate way in which Fitzgerald allows Nick to perceive Tom's relationship with Wilson has limited our response to the full play of sexuality in the story. Fitzgerald, by letting Nick have the kind of reverberating observations he does—observations increasingly integral to the way his narrator comes to look at the world— creates a kind of sexual anarchy in *The Great Gatsby*. It is a narrative of potency and impotency, of jealous sex and Platonic love, of sexuality, in fact, owing more to the simultaneity of withinness and withoutness than the narrator appears to be aware of confessing.

So far only Fiedler has cared, if in a dismissive way, to suggest that Fitzgerald's fiction is sexually ambiguous. What he notices about *Tender is the Night*, it should be noted, is perhaps ultimately more pertinent to *The Great Gatsby*:

> Indeed, the book is shot through with a thematic playing with the ambiguity of sex: Dick Diver makes his first entrance in a pair of black lace panties, and homosexuals, male and female, haunt the climaxes of the novel. "Economically," Rosemary's mother tells her at one point, "you're a boy, not a girl!" Economically! One recalls the portrait of Fitzgerald as the most beautiful showgirl in the Triangle Show.

The last reference, incidentally, is inaccurate, for it was not a single photograph taken of Fitzgerald as a showgirl, but a series of them in 1915 to publicize a Princeton musical staged by the Triangle Club, of which he was a member. Fitzgerald fell sick and couldn't make the show—even though his scholastic ineligibility would have assured his absence. According to his biographer Arthur Mizener, however, he did reappear in drag: "In February he put on his Show Girl make-up and went to a Psi

U dance at the University of Minnesota with his old friend Gus Schurmeier as escort. He spent the evening casually asking for cigarettes in the middle of the dance floor and absent-mindedly drawing a small vanity case from the top of a blue stocking. This practical joke made all the papers, but it was an inadequate substitute for the flowers he had looked forward to as "the Most Beautiful 'Show Girl' in the Triangle Club."

Of course biography is slippery ground upon which to parade an argument about sex in a writer's art, and quoting from his notebook—with a view to the same argument—may be just as elusive. Yet in view of what remains to be said of Nick's peculiar relationship with girls, the entry in Fitzgerald's posthumously published notebook, in the section called "Karacters," may encourage us to appraise further our reservations about his narrator's sometimes ambiguous account. "He," writes Fitzgerald of a "Karacter," "had once been a pederast and he had perfected a trick of writing about all his affairs as if his boy friends had been girls, thus achieving feminine types of a certain spurious originality." At this point the opening sentence of "The Rich Boy," quoted at the outset, should be recalled in order to compare Nick's narrative approach with the one in the short story: "begin with a type, and you find that you have created—nothing." These words of the narrator in "The Rich Boy" may help to explain why Fitzgerald told Perkins he felt *The Great Gatsby* was "*a man's book*"; why, in other words, he felt that his women faded out of the novel.

But if Jordan Baker, for example, is a "type" she is one whose "typical" qualities are significant in our appreciation of why Nick Carraway is attracted to them. As a champion athlete she, like Tom, is at home in the world of men. In addition, according to Nick, she has a "hard, jaunty body," a body "like a young cadet." She is, moreover, androgynously named; and her name—for someone as impressed by the shapes of cars as Nick—"combines two automobile makes" (according to one scholar), "the sporty Jordan and the conservative Baker electric." The car metaphor is dually important in the novel, for not only does it connect Tom and Wilson—a connection leading to Myrtle's death as well as Gatsby's—but it also connects Nick and Jordan soon after they meet, and here, when they part:

> We shook hands.
> "Oh, and do you remember"—she added—"a conversation we had once about driving a car?"
> "Why—not exactly."
> "You said a bad driver was only safe until she met another bad driver? Well, I met another bad driver, didn't I? I mean it was careless of me to make such a wrong guess. I thought you were rather an honest, straightforward person. I thought it was your secret pride."

"I'm thirty," I said, "I'm five years too old to lie to myself and call it honor."

She didn't answer. Angry, and half in love with her, and tremendously sorry, I turned away.

Just why they part is not clear, though to Jordan it is evident that their incompatibility derives from duplicity on Nick's part. Nick, it seems, always has been "half" attracted to women ("I wasn't actually in love, but I felt a sort of tender curiosity"; and in the passage above he confirms Jordan's final realization, that he is less honest and straightforward than he first comes on, even though critics have invariably agreed that Nick's other words, quoted as an epigraph to this paper, convey Fitzgerald's exact estimation of his narrator. Interestingly, in the manuscript version of an earlier encounter between Nick and Jordan, at Gatsby's first party, Nick half objects to what he knows is untrue (this version was later removed):

"You appeal to me," she said suddenly as we strolled away, "You're sort of slow and steady and all that sort of thing, aren't you. I mean you've got everything adjusted just right."

"On the contrary—"

"That's true though," she went on, "I used to know lots of people like you three or four years ago. But they either just stayed boys and didn't develop, or else they changed altogether."

The fact that Nick has *not* got everything adjusted just right is borne out by the observation he permits himself on the climactic evening of his thirtieth birthday: "Thirty—the promise of a decade of loneliness, a thinning list of single men to know, a thinning briefcase of enthusiasm, thinning hair." For a few last minutes—before the imminent discovery of Myrtle's mutilated body, and Tom's subsequent attempt to console Wilson—Jordan's presence seems to reassure Nick. Then the effort of living distortedly (cf. the nightmarish world of the East) leads him back to where he comes from.

Clearly it is not back to the girl out West, from whom he has escaped to come to New York. "The fact that gossip had published the banns," Nick comments early on, "was one of the reasons I had come East." Of the girl he says little, except to tell us "how, when that certain girl played tennis, a faint mustache of perspiration appeared on her upper lip." Rather secretive, the relationship is dismissed by Nick as perfunctory—and is over by chapter 4. By the end of the last chapter it seems evident that the loneliness which he prophesies on his thirtieth birthday is all Nick has to anticipate—that, and the task of recording, in his own account of the summer, a justification of his part in the events which have transpired. But does he, we come down to asking, justify everything? His activities referred to at the outset as "my personal affairs" are never really accounted for, nor is his relationship with women quite understood: unless it is accounted for in a more *subtle* way than we have hitherto suspected.

The critical problem is thus simple: is the novel plainly weak in those parts, for example Nick's relationship with McKee, his affair with Jordan, which remain shady and ambiguous; or do we give Fitzgerald the benefit of the doubt and look for other, perhaps deeper reasons to explain his apparent shortcomings in the novel? What *The Great Gatsby* seems about in part, and where it derives its suggestiveness and energy, lies in what is not accounted for, what is undisclosed. The whole of Gatsby's affair with the underworld is the obvious example of this theme and its expression. But an important statement of the theme is also, one feels, Nick's "protestation of being average and honest and open"—to put into his mouth the narrator's words in "The Rich Boy." It is not unreasonable to suppose that Nick's readiness to declare his cardinal virtue to be honesty, is deliberately intended to mislead us. This declaration tempts us into accepting everything he tells us as the whole truth, though my evidence so far is intended to suggest that the oblique or metaphoric power of the novel prevents a simple reading of the way Nick looks at the world and at himself. In any effort to understand Gatsby, there are connections ("gonnegtions") that need to be made about the story-teller himself, but which we have traditionally ignored because we have always trusted Nick as average, honest, and aboveboard.

What, then, is he hiding? An uncertain sexuality becomes an unavoidable conclusion. He is no longer simultaneously enchanted and repelled by the double vision from the window in Myrtle Wilson's New York apartment, nor is he, upon his return to the West, that "well-rounded man" he had hoped to become when "life is much more successfully looked at from a single window." His return to the West is not a solution, but a desire to escape the indecent ambiguities of conduct, "founded" on either "hard rock" or else "wet marshes." No longer tolerant of the excesses of others, Nick reaffirms his own Puritanical heritage with an extreme desire to see "the world . . . in uniform and at a sort of moral attention forever." His return is not to the girl he left behind, for he does not seem naturally inclined, in Plato's words, to marriage and procreation, and only in an oblique way is he prepared to acknowledge his own ambivalent sexuality by the association Fitzgerald allows him through the important classical echo of Petronius. (Nick, we remember, confesses his having been "rather literary" at college, and his allusion to "the shining secrets that only Midas and Morgan and Maecenas knew" is his way of introducing himself and us to the "bond business.")

Persuasive evidence of the theme of impotence and bisexuality in *The Great Gatsby* is discoverable in *The Satyricon* of Petronius, to which Fitzgerald was so sufficiently drawn that at different times he wished to call his novel after one of its characters. *Trimalchio* and *Trimalchio in West Egg* were the working titles which strongly guided Fitzgerald's composition of *The Great Gatsby* (a title which never satisfied him). Trimalchio, of course, is the name of the wealthy and vulgar host who throws the garish party in the chapter of *The Satyricon* called the "Cene Trimalchionis." What is crucial to my own discussions is not so much Trimalchio, which is what Nick calls Gatsby in the novel, as the narrator of *The Satyricon*, who attends Trimalchio's party, and whose name is Encolpios. Encolpios, who has in some way offended the fertility god, Priapus, provides what plot survives in *The Satyricon* by journeying, so scholars believe, from Marseilles east to Italy, and quite likely to the centre of the empire, Rome. Encolpios—and his name may well derive from the Greek word, *kolpos*, which, among several definitions, means vagina and womb—is a sort of Odysseus in quest of love: he is certainly a conscious parody of Odysseus, but an Odysseus both impotent and bisexual.

Now Nick (or Dud, as Fitzgerald conceived him) fails with women as Encolpios does, though not for lack of trying. Mistaken by Wolfsheim for another man who is looking for a "gonnegtion," Nick, like Gatsby, is nevertheless seeking a connection with women. Interestingly, the "gon" of "gonnegtion" is the Greek root for seed (*goné*), and one wonders, in light of Fitzgerald's subtle and conscious use of names, whether Carraway, which after all is a seed, isn't seeking "egg" in the same sense that he is portrayed as a "bond" salesman looking for business connections—from which he also flees, incidentally, rather than become tainted with the seediness (the pun seems suitable) of easy money proffered by the likes of Gatsby and Wolfsheim. There is nothing as blatantly ambivalent about Nick Carraway's sexuality as there is about that of Encolpios. Yet Fitzgerald's narrator, not unlike Petronius's, does describe in his own odyssey a parody, a parody of the American dream which rises to the poetic height we have come in *The Great Gatsby* to accept as its most indigenous quality. In Fiedler's words, "Fitzgerald's young men go east ... in quest ... of ... an absolute America; a happy ending complete with new car, big house, money, and the girl." That Gatsby and Nick *both* fail to win the girl is an interesting comment upon the subtlety of the novel. For if we begin to read through the novel with the problem of sexuality in mind, then the normal critical interpretations which focus mainly on Gatsby are seen to be too straightforward. These interpretations fail to recognize that the corruption of the novel originates not merely in Gatsby's shady business connections, but also in Nick Carraway's disingenuous sexuality. This sexuality, when peered at beside the bright and ethereal sexuality of Gatsby, or the dark and cruel sexuality of Tom, may well shed more light on why, in the novel's concluding words, "the orgiastic future . . . year by year recedes before us," and why the dud-like and impotent pursuit of that future diminishes the American dream of attaining what Anson Hunter in "The Rich Boy" tries over and over to get—the girl.

Oral Aggression and Splitting

A. B. Paulson

All critics writing about *The Great Gatsby* invariably confront that final, stunning—and by now, famous—image of the New World on the novel's last page:

> Gradually I became aware of the old island here that flowered once for Dutch sailors' eyes—a fresh, green breast of the new world. Its vanished trees, the trees that had made way for Gatsby's house, had once pandered in whispers to the last and greatest of all human dreams; for a transitory enchanted moment man must have held his breath in the presence of this continent, compelled into an aesthetic contemplation he neither understood nor desired, face to face for the last time in history with something commensurate to his capacity for wonder.

This is, in some ways, an extraordinarily pessimistic passage. Yet the sense of "vanished," "transitory," and the repetition of "last," all give way finally to an imaginative evocation for the reader of that "enchanted moment," full of promise, wonder, and awe. Accordingly, like so many other aspects of this ambiguous text, the possible meanings of Fitzgerald's words diverge, split off in two directions, and enact at another level the movement of the novel's final image: boats beating against the current.

Most literary critics attend to this duplicity, for most have suspected that it is bound up with the novel's final meaning. Again, duplicity in the text itself doubles and makes a pair with another movement toward synthesis. Needless to say, this dialect between the primitive notions of "away" and "together" may be permutated on as many levels (e. g., social, moral, spatial) as there are sensitive readers of the text. But because the assumptions through which I filter much of my own reading are psychoanalytic, I should like to discuss the text's tendency to double its

From *American Imago* 35, no. 3 (Fall 1978). Copyright © 1979 by the Association for Applied Psychoanalysis, Inc.

characters and imagery in terms of a notion Freud employed to understand certain preversions of genital sexuality: the notion of splitting. Here, the novel's contrary movement—toward synthesis—appears as a function of androgyny; that is, the mythical dream of the hermaphroditic being. Although this sort of reductive analysis will not yield the final meaning of Fitzgerald's text (he himself was right to herald it as "something extraordinary and beautiful and simple, and intricately patterned"), these psychoanalytic notions do, I think, help us to appreciate how extraordinarily intricate that pattern is.

The image of the "fresh green breast" makes a good beginning because I see both androgyny and splitting as grounded in a special relationship to the mother. But here, at the outset, most readers are likely to balk. Who is the mother in the text? Surely fathers, rather than mothers, predominate in the novel; indeed, they bracket it, beginning with Nick Carraway's father on the opening page and ending with the appearance of Mr. Henry C. Gatz for his son's funeral. Still, I would argue that mothers are conspicuous by their very absence. Partly, that void is filled by the appearance of three prominent breasts in the text, more or less consciously rendered by Fitzgerald's art. I should like to begin with these three images and the oral themes to which they are linked.

The "fresh, green breast of the new world" is not a simple image; for, while it is linked to "the last and greatest of all human dreams," its presence induces an enchanted aesthetic moment that man "neither understood nor desired." Seemingly an image of the Virgin Land, the trees nevertheless "pandered in whispers" as if the land "that flowered once for Dutch sailors' eyes" was already fallen, already deflowered and corrupted by an uneasy form of sexuality. Oddly, "trees" make a poor match with the central metaphor, "fresh, green breast." What sense does it make, we might ask, to create this correspondence between uncut—apparently feminine—trees and "the last and greatest of all human dreams"?

Earlier in the novel, confronting a second and simpler image of the breast, this enigma does not trouble us. This second image, we understand, is the original object of Gatsby's quest, and at one point he senses its presence in

> a secret place above the trees—he could climb to it, if he climbed alone, and once there he could suck on the pap of life, gulp down the incomparable milk of wonder.

Gatsby must "climb alone" because Fitzgerald's metaphor—despite its conventionality—is true to the psychic realities of nursing infants and mothers' breasts; at some deep level Gatsby pursues a source of nourishment in which the self and the world merge, fuse, and expand to colossal proportions. It is the infantile, narcissistic self which Quentin Anderson has called *imperial*; it incarnates the whole. And although Daisy, in the moment when their lips touch in a magical kiss, becomes the "perishable" "incarnation" of Gatsby's "unutterable vision," it is not surprising that "Daisy tumbled short of his dreams—not through her own fault, but because of the colossal vitality of his illusion. It had gone beyond her, beyond everything." Nor is it surprising that part of Gatsby's quest should be turned narcissistically back on himself, as Nick says, "I gathered that he wanted to recover something, some idea of himself perhaps, that had gone into loving Daisy." This double movement in which Gatsby identifies the self with the whole and then affirms both by repeating the past is, I take it, what Milton Stern responds to in the novel when he insists "that the dream is a Romantic dream in which the self replaces the very universe, in which the possibilities of self transcend any things that are needed to identify it." In his detailed analysis of the novel, Stern never explicitly links this "Romantic dream" to Gatsby's vision of "the pap of life," but his metaphors betray how astutely he responds to what we may call one of the novel's oral themes. For example, Stern pictures Gatsby as "the innocent, hungry seeker" who pursues "the object of the deepest hunger of the human heart."

If this second breast in the novel (the benign "pap of life" along with its generous supply of the "milk of wonder") allows us to better understand the nature of Gatsby's quest, it also enables us to see just why Gatsby has the sort of character he does. For if he fuses or merges in his dream with the very source of nourishment that on another level he pursues, it makes appropriate sense to see Gatsby himself as that source of supply. In other words, throughout the novel Gatsby is the great food provider on a massively generous scale. Appropriately, Fitzgerald grounds his generosity in optimism: what Nick calls at the outset, "his extraordinary gift for hope." In Erik Erikson's terms, Gatsby has an extraordinary measure of "basic trust"; that is, "a pervasive attitude toward oneself and the world derived from the experiences of the first year of life."

Finally, if one moves beyond the benign "pap of life" to the more general notion of food and eating, one can see how the mode of oral incorporation is related to one of the major thematic devices of the novel. That is, as Stern points out, "The story is organized around a series of parties. . . ." Moreover, these occasions for eating and drinking, for consuming or not consuming, eventually comprise a moral lesson in the wisdom of generosity in a world that appears less and less trustworthy. As Gale Carrithers, Jr. notes, "The novel's action is a movement from party to party, always with the hope of finding a satisfactory community. That hope is sordidly and brutally disappointed." What this alerts us to is that the imagery of "eating" in the novel is not wholly benign, and hardly innocent. For in spite of Gatsby's "gift for hope," his generous smile, and limitless optimism, there is something, Nick informs us at the outset, that "preyed upon him," something potentially destructive in the metaphor of nourishment that puns on his role as "host" to the world around him.

This other, malign oral theme in the novel is embodied in a third image of the breast. I have in mind, of course, the breast of Myrtle Wilson as Fitzgerald imagined it after the accident:

> Michaelis and this man reached her first, but when they had torn open her shirtwaist, still damp with perspiration, they saw that her left breast was swinging loose like a flap, and there was no need to listen for the heart beneath. The mouth was wide open and ripped at the corners, as though she had choked a little in giving up the tremendous vitality she had stored so long.

The emphasis on her mouth is odd here, although it runs parallel to the earlier pairing of "pap of life" with "at his lips' touch." To my mind, the "tearing open of the shirtwaist," the mouth that is "wide open and ripped," and the mutilation itself—which reduces Myrtle's ample flesh to a kind of empty shell: "swinging loose like a flap"—all this suggests an extremely primitive act of aggression. It is, I would argue, the eruption of a terrible infantile hostility from within Fitzgerald himself. One of the novel's first and most famous readers—Fitzgerald's editor at Scribner's, Maxwell Perkins—also singled out this passage, apparently objecting to it. When Fitzgerald wrote back to defend the scene, he underlined the feeling of desire that I sense in the passage, associating the verb "ripped" not with the mouth but with the torn breast. He wrote, "I *want* Myrtle Wilson's breast ripped off—it's exactly the thing, I think, and I don't want to chop up the good scenes by too much tinkering."

Fitzgerald's phrase "I don't want to chop up the good scenes" indicates how the specific image of the torn breast underlies a more general theme of destruction in the novel. He claims that he won't "chop up," yet the scenes whose form he is anxious to preserve and order have as their content a predominant pattern of chopping, breaking, smashing, and falling to pieces. As Ernest H. Lockridge has pointed out, the novel is strewn with dismembered bodies, disconnected objects, and fragments against whose background Nick Carraway, along with his drive to make connections between things and events, appears as an ordering force.

If one surveys the mass of critical literature devoted to the novel, one is apt to encounter a larger symptom of this "splitting" and consequent doubling in the text. At this more general level, the terms critics most often employ are "polarity," "doubles," "divided," "ambivalence," with "duplicity" being a special favorite. R. W. Stallman's list of doubling is a good example of Fitzgerald's technique in the novel:

> Fitzgerald shows a marked predilection for doubling identities of persons, places, and things; fashioning them by twos or pairs. Gatsby has two fathers . . . his life is divided into two parts; he is tricked by two women. Nick has two girls (one in the East and one in the West) . . . There are two timetables, two eggs, two necklaces, and so on. . . . Nothing is complete and whole as a thing in itself; nothing therefore is without imperfection.

If pressed, I might reductively argue that all of the disconnectedness in the novel is rooted in oral aggression. Yet not all of the imagery linked to such a theme is explicitly violent; quite a lot of it appears under the category of simple greed. For example, the description of Meyer Wolfsheim moves from the violent murder of Rosy Rosenthal ("they shot him three times in his full belly"); to Wolfsheim's more cautious, even fearful, style of hunger ("he began to eat with ferocious delicacy. His eyes, meanwhile, roved slowly around the room"), and finally settles on the resonant symbol of rapacity in the novel, his cuff links: " 'Finest specimens of human molars.' " Again, recall Myrtle's empty breast "swinging loose like a flap," and then consider the following seemingly small detail from earlier in the novel:

> Every Friday five crates of oranges and lemons arrived from a fruiterer in New York—every Monday these same oranges and lemons left his back door in a pyramid of pulpless halves.

It is the image of chopping, cleaving, or splitting things into "pulpless halves" that interests me. As I see it, this motif is grounded in the bodily metaphor of "biting." In associating the mechanism of division and splitting with the theme of oral aggression, I partly have in mind Erik Erikson's Basic English code-word for ambivalence and oral sadism ("an evil dividedness in human nature"). I also have in mind those British analysts, following Melanie Klein, who would see a relationship between oral aggression and a predisposition to solve later development crises by falling back upon the primitive mechanism of splitting. Again, I have in mind the defensive splitting encountered by Kohut and Kernberg in their analyses of narcissistic personalities (compare, for example, Gatsby's "platonic conception of himself" to the "grandiose self"). But finally, if I restrict my emphasis to later (primarily Oedipal) issues, it is because this gives us a chance to see how far Freud's classical formulations of *splitting* will take us toward understanding duality in the novel's structure.

The character in the novel which most critics have seen as divided or split is the narrator, Nick Carraway—and it is with him that I shall begin the remainder of my argument. Less attention has been paid to the manner in which other characters are paired and juxtaposed as if they too comprised halves of an original whole. Most interesting here, I think, is the character of Daisy Buchanan and the enigmatic quality of her voice. Finally, we shall be in a position to examine the narrator's moral stance at the novel's conclusion and relate it to one of the book's major themes: the search for identity.

There is a famous passage in the novel in which the narrator confesses the special enchantment he feels upon splitting himself into two halves. It occurs toward the end of Myrtle's party when Nick projects an imaginary self outward to the sidewalks below:

> ... each time I tried to go I became entangled in some wild, strident argument which pulled me back, as if by ropes, into my chair. Yet high over the city our line of yellow windows must have contributed their share of human secrecy to the casual watcher in the darkening streets, and I was him too, looking up and wondering. I was within and without, simultaneously enchanted and repelled by the inexhaustible variety of life.

In turn, this passage is often compared to another from the short story, "Absolution." At an early stage of *The Great Gatsby*'s composition, this story was conceived as a sketch of Gatsby's North Dakota childhood. In the story, a young boy (Rudolph Miller) confesses to an unbalanced priest several lies he has told. Adrift in his own preoccupations, the priest replies with a description of an amusement park:

> "But don't get up close," he warned Rudolph, "because if you do you'll only feel the heat and the sweat and the life."

Henry D. Piper has pointed out a number of doubling motifs in the story, "Absolution": the lie Rudolph tells is itself double, a lie about lying; Rudolph claims he is not his parents' son and therefore doubles his parents; and Rudolph has an imaginary companion or double named Blatchford Sarnemington on which he blames his bad behavior. Piper notes that the lie told during confession and the imaginary parents were both, for Fitzgerald, autobiographical; he argues that "Nick and Gatsby, like Rudolph Miller and Blatchford Sarnemington, were originally two different aspects of Fitzgerald's own personality."

Everyone seems to agree that there are autobiographical elements within Fitzgerald's novel. Everyone also agrees that there was something double about Fitzgerald's own character. Malcolm Cowley was perhaps the first to call attention, in the 1940s, to Fitzgerald's "double vision." It is this insight which Fitzgerald's biographer, Arthur Mizener, developed in an often quoted passage:

> His nature was divided. Partly he was an enthusiastic, romantic young man. Partly he was what he called himself in the "General Plan" for *Tender is the Night*, "a spoiled priest." This division shows itself in nearly every aspect of his life. The romantic young man was full of confidence about his own ability and the world's friendliness; the spoiled priest distrusted both himself and the world.

Fitzgerald himself in "The Crack-up," a series of autobiographical articles he wrote for *Esquire* in 1936—the year, by the way, in which his mother died—gives us some insight into how duality was both the source of his strength as well as his greatest weakness:

> The test of a first-rate intelligence is the ability to hold two opposed ideas in the mind at the same time, and still retain the ability to function.

Fitzgerald goes on to develop the loss of this ability, which corresponds to a "cracking" of his self, and then asks, ". . . why not slay the empty shell who had been posturing at it for four years?"

There are a number of ways in which one could pursue this juxtaposition of "true and false selves" in order to understand Fitzgerald's "crack-up" and severe depression through which he suffered in the thirties. Yet my present concern is not with the biography but with the text of the novel, and to this end it is sufficient to single out and stress his pet notion of holding "two opposed ideas in the mind at the same time." This notion is crucial because we can see how it matches two unconscious defense mechanisms for which Freud reserved the term "splitting": a split in object choice and a split in the ego. Both these notions involve relationships to women, both are tied to unconscious fantasies about the mother, and both generate—in extreme cases—perversions of genital sexuality.

We are close now to identifying the missing mother in Fitzgerald's novel, and it may be useful at this point to recall Fitzgerald's relationship to that dominating and eccentric woman who died in 1936. A passage from Mizener's biography fills in the important details:

> Even as a young boy he alternated between being ashamed of her eccentricity and devoted to her. When he got away to school and realized how

bitterly he had to suffer because of the way she had spoiled him, he was angry at her. . . . After he finished *The Great Gatsby* he started to write a novel about a matricide called *The Boy Who Killed His Mother*, on which he worked for four years without making much headway.

Norman Holland sums up both the devotion and the source of Fitzgerald's bitterness toward his mother when he writes,

> We can deduce from almost any Fitzgerald story his . . . common and vexing fears about unappeasable hungers that can only be satisfied by unreachable women or unattainable sources of riches. . . . Fitzgerald rarely talked explicitly about mothers who frustrate, but he wrote story after story about immensely powerful sources of riches, success, love, or admiration, that eventually let you down.

If the let down and frustrated little boy in Fitzgerald finally began work on a novel called *The Boy Who Killed His Mother*, then I suggest that in *The Great Gatsby* he made a trial run of embodying that fantasy in the death of Myrtle Wilson. Accordingly, Myrtle (a buxom nurturer of homeless puppies, but hardly idealized in her flamboyant vulgarity) is the first of several figures in the text who play out versions of the mother. In her death, the primitive object of rage and frustration—the "unappeasable hunger"—appears as the mutilated breast. But unless we decide that the driver of the "death car," Daisy, is oddly boyish, we must decide that Fitzgerald has not yet reached the point where a "boy" may appear explicitly as the agent in his fantasy of matricide. Of course, if we conceive of the ultimate agent in any fiction as the author, hovering above his dramatized scenes as he projects part of himself into their realization, then we might conclude that Fitzgerald derived some measure of guilty satisfaction from arranging Myrtle's death in the way he does. Recall his insistence: "I *want* Myrtle Wilson's breast ripped off."

If we look back at the scene of her death, there are details which render it disturbing in other ways. First, what strikes us is how degrading—really dirty—her death is: ". . . Myrtle Wilson, her life violently extinguished, knelt in the road and mingled her thick dark blood with the dust." Again, there is something vaguely erotic about the manner in which the two men who reach her body tear open her shirtwaist, as if the occasion were really a sexual assault. Even the description of the car striking her ("the one comin' from N'York knock right into her") has an erotic ring to it. Partly this is a function of the phallic role the automobile plays in the fantasy life of Americans—compare Gatsby's magnificent vehicle. But more important, it is a function of Fitzgerald's earlier description of adult sexuality in the novel. Especially in the relationship between Myrtle and Tom Buchanan, sexuality is rendered in terms of aggression, dominance, and victimization.

Tom first appears in the novel described in phallic terms. There is a moment in that passage when Fitzgerald teasingly moves our attention from his open legs, to his eyes, then down to his boots, up to the boot lacings, then up again, as if he was about to describe the phallus itself:

> Tom Buchanan in riding clothes was standing with his legs apart on the front porch. . . . Two shining arrogant eyes had established dominance over his face and gave him the appearance of always leaning aggressively forward. Not even the effeminate swank of his riding clothes could hide the enormous power of that body—he seemed to fill those glistening boots until he strained at the top lacing, *and you could see a great pack of muscle shifting* when his shoulder moved under his thin coat. It was a body capable of enormous leverage—a cruel body (emphasis added).

Fitzgerald's little joke here—he betrays it with the phrase "effeminate swank"—is that for all his power, Tom is the sort of man who can exercise his potency only if he is with a certain kind of woman. Myrtle Wilson is such a woman; Tom's chambermaid in Santa Barbara is another. Daisy describes such girls as "common but pretty." And it is the aggressive pursuit of such "common" women that Freud called a "psychical debasement of the sexual object." A man like Tom conceives of the sexual act as something degrading and potentially violent; therefore, he seeks out "a woman who is ethically his inferior, to whom he need attribute no aesthetic scruples, who does not know him in his other social relations and cannot judge him in them." But this figure of the woman as prostitute only exists in tension with another sort of woman to whom such men remain devoted. This, explained Freud, is a woman of "a higher kind," respected, even overvalued, but who is sexually forbidden. Both, however, taken together, actually comprise the mother who—because she has been split as an object—can be simultaneously preserved as an unreachable, respected woman, at the same time as she is possessed and degraded as a sexual object.

If Myrtle Wilson stands as the degraded half of this split image of the mother, then Daisy Buchanan—especially from the narrator's point of view—represents her counterpart: the unreachable, idealized mother. Indeed, Daisy is the only biological mother in the novel, while the emotional distance she places between herself and her daughter as she retreats from the business of childrearing only emphasizes how aloof and unreachable she is as a maternal figure. Fitzgerald pictures her "high in a white palace the king's daughter, the golden girl." But Daisy's ostensible "girlishness" only betrays the unconscious fantasy that Gatsby projects out of early adolescence and then internally pursues with outstretched arms. For Daisy is really a "first love" to which he remains so intensely faithful that we wonder if it is not some earlier woman—that *first* "first love" of all little boys—to whom he is so fanatically devoted.

More recent analysts have expanded Freud's notion of a split mother. Jeanne Lampl De Groot pointed out that

> the admired and honored woman is the mother-image of the period of the oedipus complex. She is the heiress to the great love of little Oedipus for Jocasta. The degraded sexual partner, on the other hand, is heiress to the image of the mother of the pre-oedipal phase; she has inherited the intense hostility that the little boy may have felt for her. That hostility, in turn, partly stems from his early ambivalence toward the mother . . .

If we sort Daisy and Myrtle into the categories of Oedipal and pre-Oedipal mothers, then several things become clear. First it explains an odd vacuum placed just at the point where Gatsby finally reaches and possesses the unreachable woman. "The worst fault in it," Fitzgerald wrote after the novel was published, "I think it is a BIG FAULT: I gave no account (and had no feeling about or knowledge of) the emotional relations between Gatsby and Daisy from the time of their reunion to the catastrophe." I would argue that Fitzgerald "had no feeling about or knowledge of" this relationship because, as the forbidden possession of a forbidden object, it is simply "unimaginable."

Seeing the "nice girl," Daisy, as an Oedipal mother also makes clear our response to Gatsby's death, which in the novel is called "accidental" yet which nevertheless has a kind of tragic inevitability to it. Gatsby must die because his offense is severe: he has possessed the mother. And he is killed by two of the several father figures scattered throughout the novel; that is, by Wilson in collusion with Tom. Tom is particularly good as a pivotal character in the novel (one who will play the role of "bad boy" who pursues Myrtle as a "bad mother," as well as the role of threatening Oedipal father), because he is chronologically about the same age as Nick Carraway, yet his wealth and power make him superior as a "man," yet who still functions emotionally and intellectually as a child. Again, Wilson in the early part of the novel is characterized as a child until the point at which he dominates and possesses Myrtle by locking her in her room. Throughout the novel, one might say, the male characters struggle toward manhood—and fatherhood—by fighting for possession of women. It is, for example, just when Wilson locks Myrtle up that Tom pays him an ambiguous compliment; he says Wilson looked "as if he just got some poor girl with child." Thus it is Wilson, as weak father magically become potent, inspiring moral strength from the Waste-

land God Dr. Eckleburg, and guided by Tom's directions, that finally—
gun in hand—takes revenge on Gatsby for his Oedipal crime.

There is another elaboration of Freud's notion (splits in object
choice) that will take us one step closer to understanding the manner in
which Daisy and Myrtle function as Oedipal and pre-Oedipal mothers.
First, we can add that unworthy, degraded women are seen as castrated
in the unconscious. This is one dimension of that abrupt nightmarish
moment when Tom, at the end of the raucous party, breaks Myrtle's
nose. More important, it is, I think, the final reason why Myrtle's death
makes us so uncomfortable. The breast "swinging loose like a flap" is
also a kind of symbolic castration that stamps her as debased. Now, the
correlative notion, that the Oedipal mother (and here I mean Daisy) is
not castrated, requires some explanation. For here we cross over the realm
of objects that are split to a second meaning of Freud's term: splits within
the ego.

Briefly, to fill in the theory, there is a class of neurotic disorders
activated by castration anxiety (i. e., homosexuality, exhibitionism, trans-
vestitism, and fetishism) which all revolve around the dream of the hermaphrodite; that is, the woman with a penis. Freud traced this idea back
to a common misconception in children's ideas about sexuality. Most
children, he argued, discard this belief under the pressure of reality. But
others, for a number of reasons, cling to this old vision because they
cannot tolerate the notion—again a mistaken one—of castrated beings
in the world. This fear is the source of terror that so called "phallic
women" (the Medusas and witches riding broomsticks) hold for men.
Such women are perceived as castrated in spite of the symbolic phalluses
they exhibit. Now there is another sort of "phallic woman" whose effect
is somewhat different. That is to say, the woman reassuringly endowed—
at the unconscious level—with an imaginary phallus which then makes
her tolerable as a sexual partner. Individuals who entertain this fantasy
in order to make their sexual objects acceptable must at once affirm and
deny that women possess such an organ. This is, they must have that
ability prized by Fitzgerald "to hold two opposed ideas in the mind at
the same time, and still retain the ability to function." To do this, in
Freud's terms, there must occur a split in the ego. I shall argue, then,
that the unconscious dynamics which underlie genital perversions, if
applied to imagery, events, and characters in the text, make sense of
much that otherwise remains inexplicable. Whether or not these notions
say anything about Fitzgerald's own character is simply a difficult question because Freud later broadened the notion of splitting in a way that
suggests unconscious defenses in general and because the sublimating
role of fantasy in artistic works is not really well understood.

In *The Great Gatsby*, the one character who seems to have this ability to split himself into two halves, to be "simultaneously enchanted and repelled," is the narrator, Nick Carraway. It is appropriate, then, that Nick will choose for "his girl" the hermaphroditic Jordan Baker. Lionel Trilling was the first to note that Jordan was "vaguely homosexual." It is partly her disinterest in men that gives this impression, partly the punning symbolic resonance of her golf clubs and balls, but mostly—as with Tom Buchanan—it is a matter of posture, of her whole body really. Recall Nick's first careful look at her: he says, "I enjoyed looking at her. She was a slender, small-breasted girl, with an erect carriage, which she accentuated by throwing her body backward at the shoulders like a young cadet." This motif of "the soldierly girl" is one which Otto Fenichel has linked to a fantasy in which the "girl" plays the unconscious role of phallus. I single out the motif because it appears elsewhere in Fitzgerald's fiction. For example, lesbians whose bodies are described with phallic imagery figure prominently in the story "World Fair"—a story which appeared posthumously and which is the only published chapter from the aborted novel, *The Boy Who Killed His Mother*. Just as in the phallic interpretation I am urging in regard to Jordan Baker, the women in "World Fair" are described in terms of their posture: "their heads above their black tailored suits waved gracefully at him like cobras' hoods or long-stemmed flowers in the wind." Later, when the protagonist takes the least masculine of the girls home to her apartment, he opens the bathroom door only to find her sitting on the toilet waving a small pistol in her hand. Such women fascinate the protagonist, yet they also disgust him: "He hated her for entangling him in this sordidness. . . ." Similarly, Nick has a knack for getting "entangled" in sordid affairs, and involved with women like Jordan who turn out to be vaguely threatening because they are dangerous.

But if Jordan is in some sense a phallic woman in the novel, Fitzgerald twins her with Daisy so many times that it is tempting to search for phallic characteristics in her as well. As the "golden girl" for example, she is the perfect woman; that is, as Oedipal mother, unmutilated, un-castrated. But unlike Jordan, it is not posture that Fitzgerald employs to characterize Daisy, rather it is the mysterious quality of her voice. Now it happens that there are a number of psychoanalytic case histories in which the voice of a woman played the unconscious role of "female phallus." If this unconscious equation between the voice and the her-maphroditic ideal seems farfetched, one need only recall the fascination with which eighteenth-century Western Europe regarded the castrati in Italian opera. Appropriately, in Daisy's case, her voice has the power to subdue men, to make them lean toward her. The repeated imagery which

Nick employs is that "It was the kind of voice that the ear follows up and down." If this up and down rhythm in the voice, along with the similarities to Jordan Baker, as well as some of the less than "fresh" associations to the name of Daisy itself (one thinks of homosexual slang and Fitzgerald's link between "cobras' hoods" and "long-stemmed flowers")—if all these indicate that Daisy at some level functions as a girl-phallus, then it may make clear one of the most enigmatic scenes in the novel. I have in mind the one scene set in Gatsby's bedroom to which Nick is again an enchanted and repelled observer. Here Gatsby flings out his many-colored shirts into a "soft rich heap" that mounts higher with a kind of erotic but uncomfortably fetish-like intensity, until a climax is reached:

> Suddenly, with a strained sound, Daisy bent her head into the shirts and began to cry stormily.
> "They're such beautiful shirts," she sobbed, her voice muffled in the thick folds. "It makes me sad because I've never seen such—such beautiful shirts before."

I've never been able to make much sense out of what Daisy says in this scene. But the significance may all lie in the dramatization (the "strained sound," the "bent head," the "crying," "sobbing," and "voice muffled in the thick folds") in which Gatsby, uniting fetish with his girl-phallus, provokes what amounts to an ejaculation. After a morning of anxious doubt, Gatsby has found a triumphant means for at once possessing and preserving the unreachable woman.

Up to this point, in the theoretical groundwork of my argument, I have emphasized two developmental stages: the oral sadistic and the Oedipal. That is, I have tried to indicate that the mechanism of splitting as a means for dealing with Oedipal configurations in the novel is rooted in an oral predisposition (embodied in the text's imagery) to incorporate and cleave. Anyone familiar with the methodological usefulness of applying this developmental bias to literature is likely to ask how the anal stage functions in what amounts to a multi-layered configuration of fantasies and defenses. For the answer, I return to examine one last time the novel's narrator and the quality of moral judgments that he makes.

Nick's moral judgments turn out to be oddly rigid ones, or rather, the novel is so structured that everything sorts easily into either bad or good. "Good" turns out to be orderly: "When I came back from the East last autumn I felt that I wanted the world to be in uniform and at a sort of moral attention forever." Good is also clean, like "real snow, our snow," or like the "wet laundry stiff on the line." These are the images associated with Nick's decision to go back home. "I wanted to leave things in order," he says, "and not just trust that obliging and indifferent sea to sweep my refuse away." The bad characters are finally dirty like their money: they "let other people clean up the mess they had made." They are all "a rotten crowd," the "foul dust that floated in the wake of his dreams."

If we juxtapose Nick's final division of the world into black and white, disorderly and clean, with his retreat from adult sexuality on several fronts, then I believe we can see how his return to the Midwest is really a movement back through time, against the current, back even further than the memories of returns from prep school or college at Christmas time. I suggest that he retreats from the threatening complexities of the Oedipal stage to the more orderly solutions of the anal one—from the Oedipal complex to its negative, in which one loves the father, submitting to him in a passive, feminine manner. In this setting, one of the important morals of the novel is that although you can never trust women, you can, in some ways, trust fathers. One can, for example, submit to the lessons of a Dan Cody. Even a weak father like Henry C. Gatz can be counted upon for his loyalty and fumbling love when everyone else has deserted you. This is in some ways touching, but it is an insight about fathers that is flawed by the motives in reaching it; for, Nick is driven back into his father's arms, not simply out of love, but also out of a fear of women and a hatred of his mother as a rival. In developmental terms, Nick has taken two steps forward from orality, and one step back—settling in the stage where bodily functions are androgynous because they are sexually undifferentiated.

Nevertheless, at the end of the novel, Nick has made a number of decisions, and in doing so he has delimited and defined the boundaries of his self. In choosing to go back home, in recognizing that "this has been a story of the West, after all," in turning his back on all the characters except one so that finally he found himself "on Gatsby's side, and alone," he has managed—though here one is asked to stretch and distort Erikson's term—to consolidate an identity. It is an identity based on rather expensive compromises: for example, he looks forward at the age of thirty to "a decade of loneliness, a thinning list of single men to know." Yet because the novel is about identity, about leaving home and venturing into a world of adults, about choosing a profession, about choosing a sexual role to play as well as a partner to love, it is a novel that surely appeals on several deep levels to the problems of adolescent readers. Here perhaps, its morality is satisfying in its simplicity: things sort easily into good and bad, while those judgements that appear more complex actually involve ambivalent affirmations of opposites. If novels have the power to teach, then *The Great Gatsby* instructs adolescents in the wisdom of postponing maturity, perhaps indefinitely, because the larger world is corrupt and its sexuality degrading and unfulfilling.

What then does the image of the "fresh, green Breast" signify? Several things, because as a symbol it is overdetermined; that is, it performs "multiple functions" within the text. At the level of Fitzgerald's cultural theme (the vanished American Dream), it does stand for the Virgin Land, soon to be torn and ravaged by the greedy and devouring eyes for whom it flowers. At another level—one at which we would emphasize the mixture of masculine and feminine images in the metaphor's development—it is not a breast at all; rather, it belongs to a cluster of androgynous images which all promise reassurance in the face of vexing fears about gender and sexual identity. Last, it is an image of oral trust, the one thing salvaged from the novel's debris and which stands for Gatsby's "extraordinary gift for hope." And here, despite my reservations about Nick's moral retreat, the emphasis is probably right. For this is Gatsby's story after all, and like him we do, in an important sense, "repeat the past." Accordingly, the basis for hope and trust is not out there like some "orgiastic future that year by year recedes before us"; but rather, it is what psychoanalysts would call "a good internal object," an inner sense of "basic trust" which we carry with us toward identity and beyond. A trust which assures us a measure of confidence and vitality in that quest.

The Great Gatsby

Brian Way

The power of a great novel often depends, more than anything else, upon the firmness and suitability of its underlying structure. "On this hard fine floor," Henry James wrote in his Preface to *The Awkward Age*, "the element of execution feels it may more or less confidently *dance*." A novelist cannot hope to compensate by mere "treatment" for "the loose foundation or the vague scheme." He can best avoid this kind of weakness by making his work express as far as possible the necessities of dramatic form: "The dramatist has verily to *build*, is committed to architecture, to construction at any cost; to driving in deep his vertical supports and laying across and firmly fixing his horizontal, his resting pieces." If a novel is to have this secure basis, it should be written, like a play, in scenes; and each scene should have a definite shape and a precise location—those qualities we associate with theatrical performance.

The most striking formal characteristic of *The Great Gatsby* is its scenic construction, and Scott Fitzgerald himself, as we have seen, spoke of it as a "dramatic" novel. In this respect, it shows extraordinarily close affinities with the theory and practice of James's later fiction. James's vivid account of the little diagram he drew in order to explain the structure of *The Awkward Age* to his publisher, corresponds exactly with what we find in *Gatsby*:

> I drew on a sheet of paper . . . the neat figure of a circle consisting of a number of small rounds disposed at equal distance about a central object. The central object was my situation, my subject in itself, to which the thing would owe its title, and the small rounds represented so many distinct lamps, as I liked to call them, the function of each of which would be to light with all due intensity one of its aspects . . . Each of my "lamps" would be the light of a single "social occasion" in the history and inter-

From *F. Scott Fitzgerald and the Art of Social Fiction.* Copyright © 1980 by Brian Way. Edward Arnold, Ltd., 1980.

course of the characters concerned, and would bring out to the full the latent colour of the scene in question and cause it to illuminate, to the last drop, its bearing on my theme. I revelled in this notion of the Occasion as a thing by itself, really and completely a scenic thing. . . .

The "central object" of *The Great Gatsby* is clearly Gatsby himself, and the chapters of the novel are in the main a series of dramatic scenes, each illuminating some new aspect of his character and situation. The scenes are invariably "social occasions"; often they are parties, in that special sense which is so fundamental to Fitzgerald's understanding of the 1920s. Chapter 1 is built around the dinner party at the Buchanans' at which Nick Carraway discovers the subtle charm and the inner corruption of Daisy and of the American rich—the woman and the class which Gatsby has made the object of his dreams. Chapter 2 presents the "foul dust" that floats in the wake of his dreams. It opens with a poetic and atmospheric evocation of the valley of ashes, but its main source of energy is once again dramatic—the raucous Prohibition-style party in Myrtle Wilson's apartment. In chapter 3, Nick visits one of Gatsby's own parties for the first time, and begins to understand the equivocal nature of the latter's creative powers—his capacity to mix the beautiful with the vulgar, the magical with the absurd. Chapter 4 functions like an act in two scenes, each revealing a contrasted aspect of Gatsby's identity: the lunch in New York, at which Nick meets Meyer Wolfsheim and has a glimpse of Gatsby's underworld connections; and the tea during which Jordan Baker tells him the story of Gatsby's wartime affair with Daisy. The dramatic focus of chapter 5 is the tea party at Nick's house, when Gatsby and Daisy are reunited; and in chapter 6 Nick attends a second party at Gatsby's, at which Daisy herself is present. Chapter 7, like chapter 4, is an act in two scenes: the lunch party at the Buchanans' where Tom realizes for the first time that Daisy and Gatsby are lovers; and the abortive cocktail party at the Plaza Hotel in New York, where Tom not only ends the affair, but succeeds in destroying Gatsby's "platonic conception" of himself. Only in the last two chapters does Fitzgerald largely abandon the dramatic method, and, even here, some of the most vivid moments depend on effects which are scenic in character—Mr. Gatz's arrival at Gatsby's house, Nick's second meeting with Meyer Wolfsheim in New York, and Gatsby's funeral.

Nick Carraway is a key element in the success of this scheme, indeed he is no less vital to the structure of *The Great Gatsby* than to its tone and meaning. He is both stage manager and chorus, recreating situations in all their actuality, and at the same time commenting upon them. Sometimes he even devises the action—contrives the circumstances by which the actors are brought together on the stage: it is he who arranges the reunion of Gatsby and Daisy. Nick has a further value from the structural point of view: through him, Fitzgerald is able to maintain a kind of flexibility which James considered impossible in the dramatic mode of fiction. James believed that, in order to benefit fully from the firmness of dramatic construction, the novelist was compelled to relinquish the privilege of "going behind" the action so as to analyse and comment upon it. But, thanks to Nick Carraway, Fitzgerald has the best of both worlds: he moves from the dramatic concentration of "the scenic thing" to the rich texture of narrative without the smallest effect of incoherence or inconsistency.

This principle of construction affects every aspect of Fitzgerald's artistry: in particular, the language of *The Great Gatsby* often rises at moments of intensity to the level of dramatic poetry; and the element of social comedy, which gives the novel its predominant tone and colouring, always finds expression through specifically theatrical effects of action and spectacle. The structure of a dramatic novel, however, is not an end in itself: each scene, to use James's metaphor, is a lamp illuminating a central object, and it is this object which must remain the reader's primary concern. For this reason, a scene-by-scene analysis is by no means the best way to approach *The Great Gatsby*, and a thematic treatment is far more likely to bring out the true nature of Gatsby himself. I shall therefore discuss his situation and character from three points of view: the external social reality—the way of life of the American rich— by which he has been deluded and betrayed; the texture of his inner imaginative life, which becomes, in Fitzgerald's hands, an image of the romantic sensibility and its maladies; and his dramatic identity—his essentially comic nature.

The evolution of Gatsby's dream is the history of his involvement with a social class, the American rich. The turbulent imaginings of his adolescence first take shape in the scheme of self-advancement which he draws up in imitation of Benjamin Franklin and Horatio Alger. At this time, he has a plan to make himself rich, but no clear mental picture of what wealth and success would be like. This gap is partially filled when Dan Cody's yacht anchors off the Lake Superior shore, and Gatsby meets Cody himself. At once Cody, the Western tycoon, who is spending his money in the flamboyant style of the Gilded Age, becomes Gatsby's image of the wealthy and successful man. He changes his name from Jimmy Gatz to Jay Gatsby in an attempt to embrace this new conception in all its aspects. Cody's swagger is the basis of his own social style, and, like the former, he sees the acquisition of wealth as essentially an activity of the frontier—if not the actual geographical and historical frontier, then the no-man's-land between business and criminality.

As well as an image of himself, however, Gatsby needs an image of something beyond him to which he can aspire, and this final stage in his imaginative development is completed when he meets Daisy during the War and becomes her lover. When he kissed her for the first time, he "wed forever his ineffable vision to her perishable flesh": from that moment, she was the substance of his dream, and "the incarnation was complete." In his eyes, she is intensely desirable both as a woman and as the symbol of a way of life:

> Gatsby was overwhelmingly aware of the youth and mystery which wealth imprisons and preserves, of the freshness of many clothes, and of Daisy, gleaming like silver, safe and proud above the hot struggles of the poor.

Daisy's charm involves a subtle fusion of two powerful sources of attraction, sex and money: one might say that, in her, money becomes sexually desirable. This quality is concentrated in her voice, the one facet of her beauty which can never fall short of Gatsby's dream. As Nick Carraway reflects, when he leaves them alone together for the first time after their five year separation, "I think that voice held him most, with its fluctuating, feverish warmth, because it couldn't be overdreamed— that voice was a deathless song." Nick's tone surrounds the metaphor of song with an aura of high romance, but it is Gatsby himself who uncovers the secret of those elusive cadences, when he remarks with impressive simplicity that "her voice is full of money." Many American novelists, including Henry James, Edith Wharton and Theodore Dreiser, were well aware that a beautiful woman may contain within herself all the beguiling characteristics of a social class, but no one apart from Fitzgerald has ever found so felicitous an image for the interior music of wealth.

Gatsby is incapable of seeing the American rich in any other way, but Fitzgerald, through Nick Carraway, makes us equally aware of their shortcomings from the very beginning of the novel. His introductory portraits of Daisy and Tom Buchanan are sketched in with delicate irony. Nick is half-dazzled by their wealth, and yet knows that their lives are pervaded by an atmosphere of rootlessness and futility. Since their marriage, they have "drifted here and there unrestfully wherever people played polo and were rich together"—a year in France, a season or two on Chicago's North Shore, and now a summer on Long Island. Tom's discontent seems an expression, in part, of his permanent immaturity. He had been a great football star at Yale, "a national figure in a way, one of those men who reach such an acute limited excellence at twenty-one that everything afterwards savours of anticlimax." Nick suspects that he will "drift on forever seeking, a little wistfully, for the dramatic turbulence of some irrecoverable football game."

These weaknesses are serious enough, but worse is to follow, and when Nick accepts Daisy's invitation to dinner he quickly learns the full extent of the Buchanans' corruption. Their failure is presented as the failure of a civilization, of a way of life. Nick Carraway imagines that he will find among the sophisticated Eastern rich, the high point of American civilization. The expanse of the Buchanans' lawns, the graciousness of their house, the formality of dinner, the poised, confident social tone give all the outward signs that a high civilization has been achieved. Nick contrasts the occasion with parties in the Middle West, where people hurry from one phase of the evening to the next in a state of "continually disappointed anticipation" or in "sheer nervous dread of the moment itself." "You make me feel uncivilized," he says to Daisy, "can't you talk about crops or something." At once he is ludicrously disillusioned by Tom, who is provoked by Nick's remark into an incoherent account of a book he has just read which "proves" that "civilization—oh, science and art, and all that" is threatened by the rise of the coloured races. To our sense of the restlessness and futility of their lives is now added an element of brutality and arrogance. A telephone call from Tom's mistress, and a tense whispered quarrel with Daisy offstage on which Jordan Baker eavesdrops shamelessly, conclude the scene. The rottenness of these people is conveyed with a fine sense of comedy.

Nick's disappointment has already been prefigured poetically in his first glimpse of the Buchanan household:

> A breeze blew through the room, blew curtains in at one end and out the other like pale flags, twisting them up toward the frosted wedding-cake of the ceiling, and then rippled over the wine-coloured rug, making a shadow on it as wind does on the sea.
> The only completely stationary object in the room was an enormous couch on which two young women were buoyed up as though upon an anchored balloon. They were both in white, and their dresses were rippling and fluttering as if they had just been blown back in after a short flight around the house.

The house, the draperies, the young women themselves, seem positively airborne upon Nick's romantic sense of expectation, until Tom enters: "Then there was a boom as Tom Buchanan shut the rear windows and the caught wind died out about the room, and the curtains, and the rugs and the two young women ballooned slowly to the floor." Tom brings everything quite literally down to earth. There is no more impressive instance of how much Fitzgerald's fiction gains from his sense of the specifically poetic possibilities of the novel. And, as I have already suggested . . . we are dealing here with dramatic poetry, not the large abstractions of symbol and myth. In a way which is both subtler and more flexible, the local effects of language are finely adapted to the immediate demands of the scene, the moment.

The element of physical brutality in Tom Buchanan's character is insisted upon from the beginning. An arrogant stare; a manner which is both supercilious and aggressive; "a great pack of muscle shifting when his shoulder moved under his thin coat," these are the details of his appearance which catch our attention. His brutality is constantly breaking through the veneer of his surface gentility, just as the movements of his "cruel body" show under the "effeminate swank" of his riding clothes. At that first dinner Daisy displays a finger he has bruised in some domestic tussle; he breaks Myrtle Wilson's nose with a singularly efficient application of force; and he takes a vindictive pleasure at the end in setting Wilson on Gatsby.

Tom's style of physical dominance, his capacity for exerting leverage, are not expressions merely of his individual strength but of the power of a class. Fitzgerald does not make the mistake of imagining that because the rich are corrupt, they must necessarily be weak. That fallacy was to be a part of the sentimentality of the 1930s—as we see in *The Grapes of Wrath*, where the rich appear as impotent scared little men hiding behind barbed wire and hired guns. Tom Buchanan is a far truer representative: he draws on the sense of self-assurance his money and position give him as directly as he draws upon his bank account. The consciousness that, in contrast to himself, Gatsby is "Mr. Nobody from nowhere," gives him a decisive psychological advantage in their struggle over Daisy.

The rich have subtler styles of dominance than the brute power of Tom's money or of his pampered athletic body. One of these appears in the behaviour of Jordan Baker when Nick first sees her stretched out at full length on the sofa in the Buchanans' drawing room. She takes no apparent notice of his entrance, but maintains a pose of complete self-absorption as if she were balancing some object on her chin. Far from resenting her discourtesy, Nick feels almost obliged to apologize for having interrupted her. After he and Daisy have chatted for a few moments, Daisy introduces Jordan to him:

> Miss Baker's lips fluttered, she nodded at me almost imperceptibly, and then tipped her head back again—the object she was balancing had obviously tottered a little and given her something of a fright. Again a sort of apology arose to my lips. Almost any exhibition of complete self-sufficiency draws a stunned tribute from me.

This was the quality Fitzgerald had been trying to isolate in the character of Dick Humbird in *This Side of Paradise*. By the time he wrote *The Great Gatsby*, he had learnt enough about the novel of manners to be able to make such subtle notations with complete success. In terms of dramatic conflict, these are the forces which defeat Gatsby, although clearly there are self-destructive potentialities in his own romanticism.

By the end of his dinner party at the Buchanans', Nick Carraway is already disillusioned with the American rich. He is forced unwillingly to observe the violent contrast between their opportunities—what is implied by the gracious surface of their existence—and the seamy underside which is its reality. In the Buchanans—and in Nick's reactions to them—we see once more how completely the American upper class has failed to become an aristocracy. Nick's disappointment is so sudden and complete that the episode has an effect of comic anticlimax. The chapter ends, however, not with his small disappointment but with Gatsby's first appearance. Gatsby is still totally committed to his dream: he stretches out his arms in a great yearning gesture, across the dark waters of the bay towards the green light at the end of Daisy's dock. He never discovers how he has been betrayed by the class he has idealized, and, for him, the failure of the rich has disastrous consequences.

Gatsby's unique quality is his capacity to dream—

> Some heightened sensitivity to the promises of life, as if he were related to one of those intricate machines that register earthquakes ten thousand miles away . . . an extraordinary gift for hope, a romantic readiness such as I have not found in any other person and which it is not likely I shall ever find again.

His tragedy lies in the impact of reality upon his dreams: neither the circumstances of his own life, nor the pseudo-aristocratic style of the American rich to which he aspires, offer him anything "commensurate with his capacity for wonder." Most of the ironies of his situation arise from the balancing of illusion against reality. The clearest, though by no means the most important of the ways by which Fitzgerald gives poetic substance to this duality is that of creating two settings with strongly contrasted atmospheres. The glittering palaces on Long Island Sound are set against the ash-heaps on the outskirts of New York. Gatsby's dreams are concentrated upon the former; the sordid realities which shatter his illusions and destroy his life lurk among the latter. Among the ashes, in or near Wilson's garage, Tom's rottenness and Daisy's cowardice are fully revealed; while Wilson himself, the ash-grey phantom gliding on Gatsby's track, is a singularly appropriate instrument for murder—there is after all nothing more dangerous than the hatred of the mean-spirited.

The ironic relation between illusion and reality in Gatsby's situation is conveyed most interestingly, however, by the actual language of the novel. Fitzgerald takes some of his own most vicious forms of writing—his journalistic chatter, his false rhetoric, and the cheap style of his poorest magazine fiction—and turns them into something which is artistically satisfying. It is a strange process of transmutation, by which styles that seem fitted only for crude and vulgar sentiments are, paradoxically, made to carry subtle shades of meaning and emotion. The bad writing produced with uncritical facility in the inferior pieces is here employed with conscious and elaborate artistry. An obvious and highly successful example is the list of "the names of those who came to Gatsby's house that summer" at the beginning of chapter 4. This is, among other things, a parody of the style of the gossip columns—of the cheap journalistic tone Fitzgerald could slip into all too easily himself. But it is more than a parody, or a mere compilation of those funny names which are a consequence of the diverse origins of Americans. It is a poetic composition (critics have often pointed to a similarity with T. S. Eliot's use of proper names in *Gerontion*) which gives expression to the social chaos of the Jazz Age. The names and scraps of rumour are interwoven to show how people are being hurried indiscriminately together in the frenetic pursuit of money and pleasure—the wealthy, the criminal, the disreputable, the pretentious, the showy and the frivolous, the rootless and the abandoned—even the respectable. The whiff of violence is in the air, and the presence of disaster is never far away. This is the foul dust that floated in the wake of Gatsby's dreams—the motley crowd that flock to the glittering and lavish entertainments he conceives at West Egg.

Fitzgerald takes this kind of writing farthest in his treatment of Gatsby's love for Daisy. Gatsby's taste in language is as flashy and overblown as his taste in cars or clothes: when he talks about his feelings to Nick Carraway, the words he uses retain echoes from many cheap and vulgar styles. Fitzgerald is able to catch these inflections in Gatsby's voice, and yet give to the paltry phrases vibrations they never had before. In order to see how this happens, it is necessary to quote an example of Fitzgerald's own worst writing, before turning to some passages from *The Great Gatsby*. For this purpose I have chosen the opening of "Love in the Night," a story which was published only a few weeks before *Gatsby* itself:

> The words thrilled Val. They had come into his mind sometime during the fresh gold April afternoon and he kept repeating them to himself over and over: "Love in the night: love in the night." He tried them in three languages—Russian, French and English— and decided that they were best in English. In each language they meant a different sort of love and a different sort of night—the English night seemed the warmest and softest with the thinnest and most crystalline sprinkling of stars. The English

love seemed the most fragile and romantic—a white dress and a dim face above it and eyes that were pools of light.

In the conversations with Nick in which Gatsby talks about Daisy, the same kind of writing is used:

> He had never been in such a beautiful house before. But what gave it an air of breathless intensity was that Daisy lived there. . . . There was a ripe mystery about it, a hint of bedrooms upstairs more beautiful and cool than other bedrooms, of gay and radiant activities taking place through its corridors, and of romances that were not musty and laid away already in lavender, but fresh and breathing and redolent of this year's shining motor-cars and of dances whose flowers were scarcely withered. . . .

In the first passage, Fitzgerald is tastelessly and embarrassingly self-indulgent; in the second the validity of his rhetoric is incontestable. It is the same style but it is now being used consciously and with controlling irony. Gatsby's feelings for Daisy, the moment he tries to define them, become the banal stereotypes of romantic magazine fiction, and so it is fitting that the language he uses should be vitiated by worn-out images and sentimental clichés. Fitzgerald indeed states this quite explicitly in the scene in which Gatsby drives Nick Carraway to New York, and tells him the story of his life. Gatsby recounts the autobiography he would like to have had—the wealthy family in the Middle West; the Oxford education; the grand tour—

> "After that I lived like a young rajah in all the capitals of Europe—Paris, Venice, Rome—collecting jewels, chiefly rubies, hunting big game, painting a little, things for myself only, and trying to forget something very sad that had happened to me long ago."
> With an effort I managed to restrain my incredulous laughter. The very phrases were worn so threadbare that they evoked no image except that of a turbaned "character" leaking sawdust at every pore as he pursued a tiger through the Bois de Boulogne.

The tale concludes with the amazing heroism of Gatsby's war service: "Every Allied government gave me a decoration—even Montenegro, little Montenegro down on the Adriatic Sea." "It was," Nick comments, "like skimming hastily through a dozen magazines."

Nick has just dismissed him as an extravagant impostor, a liar on the grand scale, when there is an astonishing volte-face: Gatsby produces the Montenegrin medal and a photograph of himself with a cricket bat (superb authenticating touch!) at Oxford. Nick veers to the other extreme—"Then it was all true": he pictures Gatsby, surrounded by tiger skins, in a palace on the Grand Canal, gazing into a chest of rubies to find relief from the "gnawings of his broken heart."

It is not "all true," of course, nor is it all imposture: it is a question of language, a question of images. From one point of view, it is of the essence of Gatsby's greatness that he can make these threadbare phrases and magazine stereotypes the vehicle for his stupendous capacity for wonder and imaginative response, in the same way as much of Fitzgerald's greatness in this novel lies in his ability to transmute a bad style into great art. From another angle, however, it is Gatsby's tragedy that the purest element of truth in his life story should be conveyed in the most false and sentimental of his words: "trying to forget something very sad that had happened to me long ago." The fusion of wonder and vulgarity is caught with superlative tact again and again in the novel.

We find an illuminating parallel to Gatsby's case in the greatest of all novels about the romantic sensibility—*Madame Bovary*. It is interesting to note that *Madame Bovary* had been much in Fitzgerald's mind during the period when he was writing *The Great Gatsby*. In an article which was syndicated to a number of newspapers, he listed what he considered to be the ten greatest novels ever written, and among these *Nostromo*, *Vanity Fair*, and *Madame Bovary* were singled out for special emphasis. When he wrote to Maxwell Perkins about last minute revisions he was making to the text of *Gatsby*, he warned him that the proof "will be one of the most expensive affairs since *Madame Bovary*." Flaubert's heroine shows the same capacity for wonder, the same restriction to banal images, and the same failure to find speech that can match the intensity of her feelings, as Gatsby does. This is particularly apparent in Flaubert's account of her affair with Rodolphe, a jaded middle-aged *roué*:

"I love you so much," she burst out. "So much I can't live without you! I long for you sometimes till my heart almost breaks with jealousy! I say to myself, Where is he now? Talking to other women, perhaps. They smile at him, he comes—Ah, no! no! Tell me there's none you care for! There are women more beautiful than I, but none that can love as I can. I am your slave, your concubine. You are my king, my idol—you are good, handsome, intelligent, strong!"

He had listened to so many speeches of this kind that they no longer made any impression on him. Emma was like any other mistress; and the charm of novelty, gradually slipping away like a garment, laid bare the eternal monotony of passion, whose forms and phrases are for ever the same. Any difference of feeling underlying a similarity in the words escaped the notice of that man of much experience. Because wanton or mercenary lips had murmured like phrases in his ear, he had but scant belief in the sincerity of these. High-flown language concealing tepid affection must be discounted, thought he: as though the full heart may not sometimes overflow in the emptiest metaphors, since no one can ever give the exact measure of his needs, his thoughts, or his sorrows, and human speech is like a cracked kettle on which we strum out tunes to make a bear dance, when we would move the stars to pity.

Emma Bovary is condemned to express herself in the enfeebled phrases of early nineteenth-century sentimental fiction, just as Gatsby uses the debased coinage of the magazines. In their predicament, both Fitzgerald and Flaubert show an awareness not only of the problems of the romantic sensibility, but, more specifically, of the agonies of the romantic artist— a sense that the artist himself is foredoomed to defeat whenever he tries to put his inexpressible visions into words. It has always been recognized that *The Great Gatsby* gives a wonderfully intimate picture of American manners in the 1920s, and that it is a profound exploration of the nature of American civilization, but no one has fully grasped the extent to which it is the great modern novel of romantic experience. In the entire history of the novel, only Flaubert has gone as deeply into the dangers and despairs of romanticism, and only Stendhal has seen as much of the comedy.

Gatsby himself is not an artist, however—unless one regards his parties as in some sense works of art—and he is certainly not aware that the language he uses is vulgar and ridiculous. For him, the most destructive aspect of romantic experience lies in a somewhat different direction: he finds that attaining a desired object brings a sense of loss rather than fulfilment. Once his dream loses its general and ideal quality and becomes localized within the confines of actuality, his life seems emptier and poorer. On the afternoon when Daisy first visits his house, they pause at a window to look out across the waters of the Sound, and Gatsby tells her that, but for the rain and mist which obscure the view, they would be able to see the end of her dock where the green light burns every night. Daisy takes his words as a movement of tenderness, and puts her arm through his, but Gatsby is far away—lost in what he has just said. His sense that the green light is no longer the central image in a great dream but only a green light at the end of a dock, is momentarily stronger than his response to Daisy herself touching him with her hand: "His count of enchanted objects had diminished by one."

This feeling is made still more explicit in the conversation in which Gatsby tells Nick how he first kissed Daisy. Gatsby has made a decisive choice—from this point onwards all his capacity for wonder is concentrated upon her. Even if she were far more remarkable than she is, she could not possibly measure up to such fabulous expectations, and the affair must inevitably end in some personal disaster for Gatsby. It is only because of their five-year separation that the catastrophe is delayed for so long—in Daisy's absence, Gatsby is able to dream and idealize once more without having to subject his visions to the test of actuality. Once he is reunited with her, ruin comes almost immediately: Her personal weaknesses and the inadequacies of the way of life she represents only serve to aggravate the self-destructive tendencies of Gatsby's own romanticism. This passage also raises once again, in a most interesting way, the question of language and the romantic sensibility. Nick Carraway, in the paragraph which follows it, comments explicitly on the way Gatsby talks, and on the difficulties he himself experiences in finding words for what Gatsby is trying to say:

> Through all he said, even through his appalling sentimentality, I was reminded of something—an elusive rhythm, a fragment of lost words that I had heard somewhere a long time ago. For a moment a phrase tried to take shape in my mouth and my lips parted like a dumb man's, as though there was more struggling upon them than a wisp of startled air. But they made no sound, and what I had almost remembered was incommunicable forever.

The sober precision of Nick's account of his own difficulties with language makes a marvellous contrast with the turgid unrestraint, the "appalling sentimentality," of the images which evoke Gatsby's first kiss. This seems to me to be the clearest evidence in the novel that the ironic use of bad writing in *The Great Gatsby* is the result of conscious artistry on Fitzgerald's part.

Gatsby's ruin is accomplished in a single afternoon, in the stifling hotel room in New York where he and Tom struggle for possession of Daisy, with Nick and Jordan as unwilling bystanders. The ease of Tom's victory shows the extent to which Gatsby's identity is an insubstantial fabric of illusions. There is no occasion on which Tom appears to greater disadvantage: his homilies on the sanctity of family life are as absurd as they are hypocritical; his manner towards Gatsby is crassly snobbish, towards Daisy disgustingly maudlin. He does not have the least conception of what exists between Gatsby and Daisy, nor the smallest understanding of the former's complex inner life, and yet he blunders, as unerringly as if he knew exactly what he was doing, into the area where Gatsby is most vulnerable. Through his crude accusations, he presents Gatsby, as if in a distorting mirror, with a picture of himself which is unfamiliar and yet horribly real. Tom forces him to realize that he does not necessarily appear to others in the forms which he assumes in his own magnificent conception of himself: to settled respectable people, perhaps even to a "nice girl" like Daisy, he is simply a vulgar *arriviste*, a bootlegger, a cheap swindler, the associate of crooks and gambling operators like Meyer Wolfsheim. Gatsby cannot survive this attack, clumsy as it is. The identity he has constructed for himself out of dreams and illusions, banal images and sentimental clichés, is so fragile that it disintegrates at a touch: " 'Jay Gatsby' had broken up like glass against Tom's hard malice, and the long secret extravaganza was played out."

After this, his dream of Daisy too begins to recede: while he watches her bedroom window all night from the grounds of her house, she seems to be moving steadily away from him; and when she fails to telephone him the next day, he is at last compelled to relinquish "the old warm world" which he has inhabited for so long. In these final moments of his life, he is forced to contemplate "a new world, material without being real," a world in which the loss of his dream changes the very quality of his perceptions. The common objects which surround him—sky, leaves, grass and flowers—come to seem unfamiliar, frightening, grotesque.

The core of Gatsby's tragedy is not only that he lived by dreams, but that the woman and the class and the way of life of which he dreamed—that life of the rich which the novel so ruthlessly exposes—fell so far short of the scope of his imagination. Daisy is a trivial, callous, cowardly woman who may dream a little herself but who will not let her dreams, or such unpleasant realities as running over Myrtle Wilson, disturb her comfort. That Gatsby should have dreamt of her, given his marvellous parties for her, is the special edge to his fate. Fitzgerald shows Gatsby watching over Daisy from the grounds of her house, on the night of the accident, imagining that she might still come to him, and that he is protecting her from her brutal husband. Meanwhile, Tom and Daisy are sitting comfortably in their kitchen over fried chicken and bottled ale, coming to a working arrangement for their future lives. There is a banal and shabby intimacy about their marriage, it is a realistic, if worthless, practical arrangement that suits their shallow personalities. Outside, in the night, stands Gatsby, the man of tremendous and unconquerable illusions, "watching over nothing."

By the close of the novel, Fitzgerald has completed his immensely difficult task of convincing us that Gatsby's capacity for illusion is poignant and heroic, in spite of the banality of his aspirations and the worthlessness of the objects of his dreams. The poignancy is conveyed through one incident in particular—that of the car which drives up to Gatsby's house one night long after he is dead. "Probably it was some final guest, who had been away at the ends of the earth and didn't know that the party was over." The heroic quality is there in his vigil in the garden, in the scale of his entertainments, the determination behind his criminality.

In the closing paragraphs of the novel there is a sudden enlargement of the theme—a vision of America as the continent of lost innocence and lost illusions. The Dutch sailors who first came to Long Island had an unspoilt continent before them, something "commensurate with their capacity for wonder." Gatsby's greatness was to have retained a sense of wonder as deep as the sailors' on that first landfall. His tragedy was to have had, not a continent to wonder at, but only the green light at the end of Daisy's dock, and the triviality of Daisy herself. The evolution of such triviality was his particular tragedy, and the tragedy of America.

It is easier to discuss Gatsby's significance and the nature of his experience, as I have done so far, than to say what kind of fictional character he is. A number of early readers of the novel including Edith Wharton and H. L. Mencken, felt that as a character he virtually didn't exist. Most later critics have evaded the problem altogether by elevating him to the status of a mythic figure. Approached in this way he becomes a symbolic abstraction, the vehicle for a few schoolbook platitudes about American history, and the question of whether or not he is a tangible dramatic and human presence conveniently disappears. If one simply reads the novel, however, his dramatic and human presence obstinately and delightfully remains:

> Gatsby, his hands still in his pockets, was reclining against the mantel-piece in a strained counterfeit of perfect ease, even of boredom. His head leaned back so far that it rested against the face of a defunct mantelpiece clock, and from this position his distraught eyes stared down at Daisy, who was sitting, frightened but graceful, on the edge of a stiff chair.
> "We've met before," muttered Gatsby. His eyes glanced momentar-ily at me, and his lips parted with an abortive attempt at a laugh. Luckily the clock took this moment to tilt dangerously at the pressure of his head, whereupon he turned and caught it with trembling fingers and set it back in place. Then he sat down, rigidly, his elbow on the arm of the sofa and his chin in his hand.
> "I'm sorry about the clock," he said.
> My own face had now assumed a deep tropical burn. I couldn't muster up a single commonplace out of the thousand in my head.
> "It's an old clock," I told them idiotically.
> I think we all believed for a moment that it had smashed in pieces on the floor.

The reality of Gatsby's character here is, overwhelmingly, comic, and it is this comic Gatsby—not a shadowy abstraction—who dominates the novel.

The only warrant for considering him as a mythic figure is given on the last page of the novel and, while it would be foolish to deny that the language of this passage is the language of myth, it should be re-membered that what Nick Carraway says here is an afterthought, an aspect of Gatsby's case perceived only after he is dead. The living Gatsby who dominates one scene after another is a creature of comedy not myth—a literary relative not of Davy Crockett but Trimalchio.

The Great Gatsby itself is best regarded as a social comedy, but the phrase doesn't perhaps sufficiently convey the extent to which the comic is the vital creative element in Fitzgerald's achievement. The term social comedy usually implies a mode of writing which is satirical and moral, and this is certainly true of his treatment of a number of characters and episodes—in particular of Tom Buchanan. But frequently his writing rises to a level of rich absurdity where comedy is not subordinated to a satirical or moral point, but is itself the point—the truly creative thing. Such a moment occurs in the episode in which Myrtle Wilson buys a dog:

> We backed up to a grey old man who bore an absurd resemblance to John D. Rockefeller. In a basket swung from his neck cowered a dozen very recent puppies of an indeterminate breed.
> "What kind are they?" asked Mrs. Wilson eagerly, as he came to the taxi-window.
> "All kinds. What kind do you want, lady?"
> "I'd like to get one of those police dogs; I don't suppose you got that kind?"
> The man peered doubtfully into the basket, plunged in his hand and drew one up, wriggling, by the back of the neck.
> "That's no police dog," said Tom.
> "No, it's not exactly a police dog," said the man with disappointment in his voice. "It's more of an Airedale." He passed his hand over the brown washrag of a back. "Look at that coat. Some coat. That's a dog that'll never bother you with catching cold."
> "I think it's cute," said Mrs. Wilson enthusiastically. "How much is it?"
> "That dog?" He looked at it admiringly. "That dog will cost you ten dollars."
> The Airedale—undoubtedly there was an Airedale concerned in it somewhere, though its feet were startlingly white—changed hands and settled down into Mrs. Wilson's lap, where she fondled the weatherproof coat with rapture.
> "Is it a boy or a girl?" she asked delicately.
> "That dog? That dog's a boy."
> "It's a bitch," said Tom decisively. "Here's your money. Go and buy ten more dogs with it."

To say that this incident illustrates the false gentility of Myrtle Wilson or the crudeness of Tom Buchanan's desires would be true but inessential. What really matters is the irresistibly joyous and liberating sense of the ridiculous which Fitzgerald conveys—that quality in literature which we call, not loosely but precisely, Dickensian. As Grahame Smith admirably expresses it in his study of Dickens apropos of Mrs. Gamp—"we recognize that we are enclosed in a magic circle of pure comedy from which it is impossible to break out with explanations of satirical intent or didactic purpose." The whole ensuing scene of the party at Myrtle Wilson's apartment is conceived on the same level of pure comedy. Nick Carraway's two encounters with Meyer Wolfsheim have the same quality. Wolfsheim isn't in the novel to give us tangible proof of Gatsby's underworld connections—the cryptic telephone calls the latter occasionally receives are enough to do that. Wolfsheim's monstrous absurdity—his nostrils, his cuff buttons, his sentimentality and his philosophy of life—is an end in itself. It is significant that Edith Wharton considered him ("your wonderful Jew") the best thing in the novel.

Fitzgerald's greatest success by far in this mode of comedy, however, is the character of Gatsby himself. It is the comic element in Gatsby which makes him seem credibly alive—which gives him an independent existence as a fictional character. We depend on Nick Carraway's testimony for much of what we believe about him. Without the benefit of Nick's wide privilege of interpretation, and the assurance of his sober integrity, we should not be able to guess at the stupendous imaginative life that lies beneath Gatsby's trivial aspirations. But we don't need Nick to tell us how funny Gatsby is—we see it for ourselves. Here, Nick no longer interprets and guarantees, he merely records—he might almost as well not be there. We should probably be less ready to take his word even for Gatsby's imagination, if Gatsby were less comic. His sole creative talent—it is one of which he is entirely unconscious—is his power to arouse wild incredulous laughter. His life has the aspect of a non-stop theatrical performance—an "unbroken series of successful gestures"; even his name, Jay Gatsby, is a farcical stunt. He does not provoke the superficial kind of laughter which is a mere brief contortion of the facial muscles; he appeals to a profound comic sense which makes life seem richer and fuller than it normally is. When one laughs at his car, his clothes, his parties, his manner, his autobiographical confidences, one is not merely amused, one is responding, through him, to the fertile, creative ludicrousness of life itself.

Gatsby's account of himself during the car ride to New York (from which I have already quoted) is one of the finest of such moments. The episode is too long to give in full, but a single detail—the way in which the car itself is described—will serve to bring out the nature of Fitzgerald's comic vision. Gatsby's car is a fantasy of colours, shapes and noises: its horn emits bursts of music; its "labyrinth of wind-shields" mirrors a dozen suns; its monstrous length is swollen with "triumphant hat-boxes and supper-boxes and tool-boxes." It is clearly not so much a means of transport as a theatrical gesture, a fantastic expression of personality, as characteristic in its way as Falstaff's belly. (Falstaff, as Grahame Smith points out is as essential as Dickens to any discussion of pure comedy.)

There are certain striking similarities between the ways in which Gatsby and Falstaff function as comic characters. One of these becomes apparent in the scene from *Henry IV, Part 2*, in which Falstaff comments on the ludicrous contrast between his tiny page and his own monstrous bulk:

> The brain of this foolish-compounded clay, man, is not able to invent anything that intends to laughter more than I invent, or is invented on me; I am not only witty in myself, but the cause that wit is in other men. I do here walk before thee like a sow that hath overwhelmed all her litter but one.

Gatsby is never consciously witty as Falstaff is—indeed he seems to be totally without a sense of humour—but he is certainly "the cause that wit is in other men." Both characters need only to exist in order to be comic.

The Falstaff parallel is illuminating in a further sense. It is usual to speak of the wreck of Gatsby's dreams as a tragedy—a statement of the case which appears to contradict the view that he is essentially a comic character. Gatsby, however, clearly isn't a tragic hero in any strict sense: if one calls his end a tragedy, one is simply giving the word the meaning it has in everyday speech—that of the sudden and shocking ruin of a human life. No inconsistency is involved if a comic character dies in this way. Falstaff is cruelly rejected by the king, and the manner of his death as narrated by Mistress Quickly is deeply moving, but these circumstances do not alter his essentially comic nature. The emotions aroused by Gatsby's death, similarly, do not negate the effect of earlier scenes.

The most successful of Gatsby's theatrical gestures are his parties. At the simple level they are fun, an aspect of the novel's meaning which is as true and as important as Nick Carraway's moral disapproval of Gatsby's guests. We are reminded once again of what Henry James and Henry Adams were forced to concede, however reluctantly—that the charm, the success, of American life is in democratic manners, even in social chaos. The corresponding failure of the aristocratic experiment—the stuffy, boorish, hypocritical life of the Buchanans—is clear enough, and throws Gatsby's achievement into sharp relief. Daisy finds—and this is perhaps the sole basis of her love for Gatsby—that there are romantic possibilities in the disorderly riot of his world totally absent from her own. Even the dissipations he offers, or condones, at his house are frank, lively and diverting—very different from Tom Buchanan's crude and furtive relaxations.

Gatsby's parties, too, are virtually his only genuine acts of creation. His dream of Daisy and the way of life she represents, whatever imaginative intensity he puts into it, is an absurd and vulgar illusion. His "platonic conception" of himself does not differ very significantly from the pattern of Dan Cody's career—the robber baron turned playboy. But his parties are triumphant expressions of that "vast, vulgar and meretricious beauty" which, as we have already seen, is one of the most characteristic manifestations of American life. When Nick tells Gatsby that his house looks like the World's Fair, and reflects that his guests "conducted themselves according to the rules of behaviour associated with an amusement park"; or when Tom Buchanan calls Gatsby's car a "circus-wagon," the implications are clearly unfavourable. And yet, taken in relation to the parties themselves, these gibes help to direct our attention to something very different: "There was music from my neighbour's house through the summer nights. In his blue gardens men and girls came and went like moths among the whisperings and the champagne and the stars."

> The lights grow brighter as the earth lurches away from the sun, and now the orchestra is playing yellow cocktail music, and the opera of voices pitches a key higher. Laughter is easier minute by minute, spilled with prodigality, tipped out at a cheerful word. The groups change more swiftly, swell with new arrivals, dissolve and form in the same breath; already there are wanderers, confident girls who move here and there among the stouter and more stable, become for a sharp, joyous moment the centre of a group, and then, excited with triumph, glide on through the sea-change of faces and voices and colours under the constantly changing light.

That Gatsby should have brought to life all this miraculous shimmering ephemeral beauty and excitement places him among the great artist-showmen of America—the architects who designed the World's Fairs and Expositions; the circus ring-masters, and the gifted mountebanks of the state and county fairs; the directors of Hollywood epics and musicals; and the scientists, astronauts and media men who, between them, turned the Apollo moon-shots into the best television entertainment ever made.

To these creative gifts, Gatsby adds the gift of comedy. His parties always seem about to bubble over into a burst of irresistible laughter. Even the mechanical housekeeping arrangements have a comic effect: the servants who toil "with mops and scrubbing-brushes and hammers and garden-shears, repairing the ravages of the night before"; the caterers who, with tempting foods, yards of canvas, and hundreds of coloured lights, turn Gatsby's gardens into an enormous Christmas tree; the crates of oranges and lemons which arrive like expected guests from New York, have their juice extracted, and leave his back door in a "pyramid of pulpless halves." When, a little later in the evening, Nick Carraway speaks of "the premature moon, produced like the supper, no doubt, out of a caterer's basket," the whole scene seems to hover between the magical and the absurd. A similar effect is obtained at the beginning of Orson Welles's *Citizen Kane*, in the newsreel which describes Xanadu—not Kubla Khan's pleasure-dome but Kane's monstrous Florida estate. A particularly felicitous touch is the reference to Kane's collection of animals—"a specimen of every animal, bird and reptile in the world—the largest private zoo since Noah's Ark."

As Nick's evocation of the atmosphere of Gatsby's parties gradually modulates into his account of the first one he actually attended, the comic element becomes more explicit. At the beginning, it is like a ripple of suppressed laughter half-heard in the general concert of sounds, but soon, like the mounting hilarity of the guests themselves, it becomes unmistakably the dominant note. It is at this phase of the evening that Nick and Jordan find the owl-eyed man admiring Gatsby's library. Then the rhythm of the party changes again—from hilarity to comic uproar: a drunken soprano performs with tears of black mascara streaming down her face, and, in the riotous finale, the owl-eyed man reappears—as the uncomprehending passenger of a car which has lost one of its wheels. The presiding genius at this scene of comic revelry is Gatsby: he surveys his departing guests from the steps of his house, his hand raised, amid the din of motor-horns in a formal gesture of farewell.

It is in this respect that he most resembles Trimalchio, a character who was very much in Fitzgerald's mind while he was writing *The Great Gatsby*. When Gatsby abruptly stops giving his parties, Nick remarks that "his career as Trimalchio was over"; and at one stage Fitzgerald actually considered *Trimalchio* and *Trimalchio in West Egg* as possible titles for the novel. Trimalchio's banquet, the longest episode in the *Satyricon* of Petronius, is one of the great comic scenes of classical literature, and has certain obvious resemblances with Gatsby's parties. Both are set in times of wealth and decadence (Petronius himself is usually—though not certainly—identified with that Petronius Arbiter described by Tacitus, who presided over the revels at the court of Nero). The guests in each case are a motley collection of adventurers and entertainers, while the two hosts are *nouveaux riches* with the uncertain taste common to that position. In both entertainments the life and virtue are comic, and both reach their dramatic climaxes in scenes of comic disorder. Gatsby's pose—aloof, dignified, ceremonial almost—is in ludicrous contrast with the turmoil of farcical misunderstandings and caterwauling motor-horns in his drive. The *débâcle* of Trimalchio's banquet has the same relation to the whole, and contains similar comic incongruities. In order to parade his wealth and liberality, he has his will brought in and read aloud. As his slaves and guests weep drunkenly, he is inspired by the thought that they can pretend the occasion is his funeral wake. He lies down on a couch as if he were the corpse, libations are poured out, and a brass band is summoned to play suitable music. But the leading performer gives such a piercing blast on his instrument that the whole neighbourhood is awakened. The fire brigade is aroused, and the guests flee in terror as the firemen rush in with their axes and buckets of water.

While it is almost certain that Fitzgerald learned something from Petronius about the dramatic organization of such scenes—about the mounting rhythms that run through huge entertainments—his comic sense is entirely his own. In Trimalchio's banquet there is no trace of that magical lightness and beauty which hover over Gatsby's parties— indeed, the tasteless display, the revolting food, the boring songs and recitations, and the fatuous practical jokes are only redeemed by the comic vitality of Trimalchio himself. Petronius's comedy is excellent, but it is straightforwardly Rabelaisian, neither very subtle nor very varied. One cannot but feel that Fitzgerald's comic sense is, by contrast, finer and more inventive. Gatsby's nature contains both grossness and delicacy; his oblique relation to his guests allows of many ironies which are outside Petronius's range; and his parties display an incomparable variety of mood and atmosphere. *The Great Gatsby* is the only work in which Fitzgerald realized the full potentialities of his comic genius, but in this one novel he equalled the masters of world literature.

Fitzgerald's vision of life in *The Great Gatsby* is a complex one: he appreciates the comic vitality of Gatsby and the grandiose scope of his romantic imagination; at the same time, there is an equally important element of moral rigour in the novel, which is most apparent in Fitzgerald's attitude to the American rich. The relation these conflicting elements have to each other has some similarities with the complex meaning of Falstaff's position in the *Henry IV* plays: the mere fact of Falstaff's existence is a creative and liberating force, and yet one cannot deny the baseness of most of what he does. As both Shakespeare and Fitzgerald recognize, these two perceptions do not cancel each other out, nor is there any convenient formula that will resolve them. Each artist seems to say in effect, life is like that—that is a part of its complexity. That this sense of complexity is so successfully conveyed in *The Great Gatsby* is due almost entirely to the figure of Nick Carraway.

Nick combines the role of stern moral critic with that of fascinated and disinterested spectator of life. Fitzgerald is careful to define these attitudes at the beginning of the novel in such a way that this double vision can be seen as a plausible expression of a single unified character.

The way in which Nick describes his ancestry—light and almost flippant as it is—suggests that the explanation may lie there. According to family tradition, the Carraways are descended from the Dukes of Buccleuch, but in reality their story begins with Nick's great-uncle, who came West in 1859, sent a substitute to the Civil War, and started the wholesale hardware business which is still the basis of their fortunes. The sense of divided loyalties is clear—to a romantic, pseudo-aristocratic ideal on the one hand, and to the standards of a sober, practical, commercial respectability on the other. It is wholly characteristic of Fitzgerald that this conflict of allegiances should be presented partly in terms of social class. Only through an aristocratic conception of man can the largest human possibilities be realized, but middle-class life is the only source of moral integrity and of stability in personal relationships.

Fitzgerald makes the same distinction in somewhat different terms in the first words of the novel. Nick Carraway recalls how his father, in a somewhat enigmatic manner, had once reminded him that "a sense of the fundamental decencies is parcelled out unequally at birth"—a superior moral sense is one of the many advantages a man inherits from being born into a good family. The awareness of this privilege has made Nick tolerant when he encounters lower moral standards in others, and his tolerance has, in turn, made him the recipient of many strange confidences. But there are times when his impulse towards tolerance and receptivity is met by an equally strong principle of moral restraint: "When I came back from the East last autumn I felt that I wanted the world to be in uniform and at a sort of moral attention for ever." Only Gatsby is exempt from Nick's recoil into disapproval—"Gatsby, who represented everything for which I have an unaffected scorn." This passage is the key to Nick's position as narrator: it explains why he is able gradually to recognize Gatsby's extraordinary qualities. It also accounts for his prompt reaction to the Buchanans—why it is that his initial fascination with their way of life turns to disgust in a single evening: "To a certain temperament the situation might have seemed intriguing—my own instinct was to telephone immediately for the police." Most interestingly of all, perhaps, Nick's self-analysis tells us why, having recognized the Buchanans' rottenness so early, he puts up with them socially for so long.

Nick's moral stand, the point at which the limits of his tolerance are reached, involves, we notice, a return from the East to the Middle Western city where his family lives. Almost at the end of the novel he remarks, "this has been a story of the West, after all" and at least part of the significance of these words is the bearing they have upon his complex moral position. The Middle West is home, the place to return to after dubious, if exciting, adventures in the East, a place where the sober, provincial, domestic virtues continue to maintain an unquestioned authority. Like the contrast in class values, this difference in regional cultures adds a further element of interest to Nick's responses.

It would be a mistake to see Nick simply as a narrator, however: he is a definite and important character. One of his functions is as Gatsby's shadow, a man who would have the same dreams as Gatsby if he could. Like Gatsby, he is a Middle Western boy who finds, after the upheaval of the War, that, "Instead of being the warm centre of the world, the Middle West now seemed the ragged edge of the universe." He comes East to make a quick fortune in the bond business and to become a part of a more sophisticated way of life. The fact that he can neither dream, nor live out the implications of his dreams, as Gatsby does, makes him a useful foil to Gatsby: by the measure of his ordinariness, we appreciate Gatsby's greatness all the more. Nick, too, pays his own modest tribute, at many points in the novel, to Daisy's charm, adding the necessary touch of credibility to Gatsby's dreams. His own half-hearted romance with Jordan Baker—a girl who, like Daisy, is careless, dishonest and "a rotten driver"—again reminds one by contrast of the stupendous scale of Gatsby's love. The only decisive step Nick ever takes towards Jordan, in fact, is on the afternoon when she tells him what she knows of Gatsby's affair with Daisy five years before in Louisville. Moved momentarily by the story of another man's love, he kisses her.

It would be absurd to attempt to sum up Fitzgerald's achievement in *The Great Gatsby* in a single concluding phrase; all one can do is to try, as I have done, to show some of the sources of its greatness. However, there is one general comment that is in place: the novel is remarkable for the extent to which it succeeds in combining imaginative power and vitality with faultless artistry. The depth and range of its analysis of American civilization, the intensity with which it evokes the life of the romantic sensibility, and the wonderful comic vision that led to the creation of its hero, are balanced and controlled by a miraculously precise attention to detail—a poet's sense of the possibilities of language. *The Great Gatsby*, in achieving this particular kind of success, is not only unique among American novels of the twentieth century, but an undoubted masterpiece of world literature.

The *Waste Land* Myth and Symbols in *The Great Gatsby*

Letha Audhuy

Most critics and readers of F. Scott Fitzgerald's novel *The Great Gatsby* have sensed at least a general thematic analogy with T. S. Eliot's poem *The Waste Land*, and one can occasionally find references to Fitzgerald's "moral wasteland." The connection between Fitzgerald's striking description of the "valley of ashes" in chapter 2 of his book, and Eliot's (and Ezekiel's) valley of dry bones, both central symbols in the two works, appears obvious. However, I would suggest, through a close reading of *Gatsby*, that the parallel goes much further than has been noticed so far; and that Fitzgerald, consciously and unconsciously, drew upon *The Waste Land* as a whole, to the point of making it the informing myth of his novel.

Before turning to the text itself, one may properly inquire whether there is any more overt evidence of this literary inspiration of the younger by the elder American writer. Research reveals Fitzgerald's acknowledgement of his debt to Conrad, principally in matters of narrative technique, but, it is true, no direct admission of Eliot as a source. However, two letters written by Fitzgerald to his Scribner's editor, Maxwell Perkins, speak of the regard of the two writers for each other's work, and offer some support for my contention. In the first letter, dated Feb. 20, 1926, Fitzgerald spoke of Eliot in these terms: "T. S. Eliot, for whom you know my profound admiration . . . I think he's the greatest living poet in any language . . . ," and the second letter, dated Oct. 19, 1933, recapitulates the first one saying:

From *Etudes Anglaises* 33, no.1 (1980). Copyright © 1980 by Didier-Erudition, Paris.

As to T. S. Eliot:
What he said was in a letter to me . . . that he'd read it [*The Great Gatsby*]
several times, it had interested and excited him more than any novel he
had seen either English or American for a number of years, and he also
said that it was the first step forward in the American novel since Henry
James.

We can surmise that Eliot was "excited" by Fitzgerald's use, in an original
poetic novel, of his own material, as if he were its spiritual godfather;
and Fitzgerald could only be gratified by this "shock of recognition" from
his eminent senior. We must recall too, the dates of publication of the
two works; *The Waste Land* in 1922, *The Great Gatsby* following hard
upon it, in 1925, which makes it plausible that Fitzgerald would have
had the meanings and motifs of *The Waste Land* fresh in his mind while
composing *Gatsby*.

But now, let us "trust the tale." In order to show that Fitzgerald
transposes Eliot's myth to an American context, giving it a specifically
American application and originality, I will study five aspects of *The
Great Gatsby*, progressing in depth from setting, social criticism, through
characters, elemental and seasonal symbols that structure the story, and
finally, the moral theme of the novel. Perhaps an examination of *Gatsby*
in this new light will help to clarify some perplexing points in the work,
about which Fitzgerald himself said: "Of all the review [*sic*], even the
most enthusiastic, not one had the slightest idea what the book was
about."

It is, first of all, the setting of *The Great Gatsby* that strikes the
reader's imagination as somehow reminiscent of *The Waste Land*, although not indeed by a strictly physical resemblance. The landscape of
the first and last parts of Eliot's poem is a "dead land" strewn with "stony
rubbish," and then a dry, rocky mountainous place of "dry bones," and
finally, an "arid plain." Fitzgerald created a new type of "waste land" (he
does use the term in chapter 2) with his "valley of ashes":

About half-way between West Egg and New York the motor road hastily
joins the railroad and runs beside it for a quarter of a mile, so as to shrink
away from a certain desolate area of land. This is a valley of ashes . . . a
fantastic farm where ashes grow like wheat into ridges and hills and grotesque gardens; where ashes take the forms of houses and chimneys and
rising smoke and, finally, with a transcendent effort, of ash-grey men, who
move dimly and already crumbling through the powdery air. Occasionally
a line of grey cars crawls along an invisible track, gives out a ghastly creak,
and comes to rest, and immediately the ash-grey men swarm up with
leaden spades and stir up an impenetrable cloud, which screens their obscure operations from your sight.

Both these desolate lands are emblematic of sterility and waste, and they underscore the main theme of each work. Eliot is of course concerned with the loss of faith and love in the modern world, while Fitzgerald explores the more limited theme of the corruption of the American dream by materialism. The rolling "fields of the republic" have become a garbage dump. Eliot's keynote of dryness becomes in *Gatsby* "dust" or "powder" which appears at strategic points of the narrative to evoke the emptiness, the "hollowness," the futility of America in the Jazz Age. This may not seem new.

However, the great sign, the eyes of Dr. T. J. Eckleburg, set above the valley of ashes is perhaps an ironic development and commentary upon Eliot's view of the modern world, a secularized waste land, in which "God is dead." In Fitzgerald's book, there is a new, but *false* god, who, the people (in the person of Wilson) believe, "sees everything." In America in the 1920s the new god was commercialism or materialism. One is reminded of the line from "Gerontion" (a poem so closely related to *The Waste Land* that Eliot wanted to use it for a prologue): "Signs are taken for wonders." Here, Fitzgerald's joke is to make an actual sign (board) into a wonder. The tone is ironic, rather than despairing, when he says: "Some wild wag set them [the eyes] there to fatten his practice and then sank down himself into eternal blindness. . . ."

Certain other details, taken in the context, seem to indicate a topographical likeness between the two "waste lands." "The valley of ashes is bounded on one side by a small foul river" which may recall the "dull canal," along "the arid plain," in which the protagonist of *The Waste Land* was fishing in vain. That is, polluted water everywhere, and so, "not a drop to drink." Resemblance, too, between the "Sweet Thames" flowing in *The Waste Land*, in autumn when:

> The river bears no empty bottles, sandwich papers,
> Silk handkerchiefs, cardboard boxes, cigarette ends,
> Or other testimony of summer nights. The nymphs are departed.

and the waters of Long Island Sound, which had borne the flotsam and jetsam of Gatsby's parties on summer nights. Gatsby's magnificent shore mansion is a kind of reincarnation of the luxurious palace seen in part 2 of *The Waste Land*, "A Game of Chess," and the "Babylonian captivity" that visitors are held in there is suggested as it is in Eliot's lines. It is Nick, Fitzgerald's narrator, who in a sense, "sits down and weeps" by the waters of the Sound at the end of the novel. (Gatsby's mansion may also represent the Fisher King's castle, as we shall see.)

But Eliot's vision takes in the urban landscape of the "Unreal city," too, a Dantesque London, where the people are leading death-in-life. In

Gatsby, Fitzgerald transmutes the same elements into a new poetry, Eliot's London Bridge becomes the Queensboro Bridge, and the "unreal city" is New York:

> Over the great bridge with the sunlight through the girders making a constant flicker upon the moving cars, with the city rising up across the river in white heaps and sugar lumps all built with a wish out of non-olfactory money.

Fitzgerald's emphasis is different from Eliot's; his city offers "the first wild promise of all the mystery and beauty in the world," and he heightens the unrealness of the unreal city, in the sense of the absurd, because in *Gatsby,* strange things happen there, and bizarre revelations are made to Nick, the narrator. In chapter 4, just before passing "over the great bridge," Gatsby has told Nick a fantastic tale of his past, and Nick's reaction is:

> "Anything can happen now that we've slid over this bridge," I thought, "anything at all . . ."
> Even Gatsby could happen, without any particular wonder.

But New York will be the realm of disillusion and death, too. As Nick and Gatsby go over the bridge, "a dead man" passes them "in a hearse," a dramatic foreshadowing of later events, Gatsby's death, and also Myrtle's.

Not only in their setting, but in their view of modern society, can parallels be drawn between *The Waste Land* and *The Great Gatsby.* The decline of civilization postulated by Eliot (. . . "you know only/A heap of broken images") is echoed in parody form, early in *Gatsby,* by Tom Buchanan. Apropos of nothing in particular, he bursts out in a violent pseudo-scientific diatribe about civilization going to pieces and the white race being submerged by the "coloured" races. The unimaginative Tom is somewhat pathetic, trying to explain a book he has just read and seems hardly to understand. Even Daisy chimes in: " 'We've got to beat them down,' whispered Daisy, winking ferociously toward the fervent sun." These hordes Daisy is ready to do battle against had already appeared in *The Waste Land:* "Who are those hooded hordes swarming/Over endless plains." Chapter 7 picks up the same theme of the decline of civilization. Again Tom is speaking:

> "Nowadays people begin by sneering at family life and institutions, and next they'll throw everything overboard and have intermarriage between black and white."
> Flushed with his impassioned gibberish, he saw himself standing alone on the last barrier of civilization.

Fitzgerald uses heavy irony here, by making Tom the adulterer the indignant mouthpiece of such "edifying" sentiments about the modern world. Although the theme of *The Great Gatsby* is indeed concerned with decline, and the perversion in America of "the last and greatest of all human dreams," and the book does conclude on a nostalgic note, yet the treatment of this theme can be parodic. One may remember the startling vision in chapter 4 of the limousine,

> driven by a white chauffeur, in which sat three modish negroes, two bucks and a girl. I [Nick] laughed aloud as the yolks of their eyeballs rolled towards us in haughty rivalry. "Anything can happen now. . . ."

Against this backdrop of the decay of civilization, the waste lands of both Eliot and Fitzgerald surround pub and palace alike. Their "hollow men" (Eliot's poem by the same name was published in 1925) come from both the lower and upper classes, the poor and the rich. Most of Eliot's modern characters are taken from low life, but lust and meaninglessness link them to the aristocrats of the Renaissance and antiquity. Fitzgerald does not limit his fable to the wealthy American upper class; he deliberately creates analogies between high and low life through the connections between Tom and his mistress Myrtle, and between Gatsby and the underworld, that correspond to Eliot's picture in "The Game of Chess." Lil could almost have served as a prototype for the vital but vulgar Myrtle; both are unhappy in marriage, too. Meyer Wolfsheim, Gatsby's friend the gambler, like Mr. Eugenides, the Smyrna merchant, represents the shady business world, "the profit and the loss." Both initiate the innocent protagonist (Tiresias and Nick) into another mysterious, corrupt world (and not into the Grail mystery).

Gatsby himself represents the "parvenu," and in the novel there are several allusions that seem to be echoes of Eliot's poem. The epigraph to *Gatsby* runs thus:

> Then wear the gold hat, if that will move her;
> If you can bounce high, bounce for her too;
> Till she cry Lover, gold-hatted, high-bouncing lover,
>   I must have you!
> Thomas Parke d'Invilliers

The reader of *The Waste Land* will remember in part 3, "The Fire Sermon":

> He, the young man carbuncular, arrives,
> A small house agent's clerk, with one bold stare,
> One of the low on whom assurance sits
> As a silk hat on a Bradford millionaire.

The gold hat or the silk hat is each time symbolic of the "nouveau riche." Oddly enough, the other illusion concerns the epigraph to the other work, that is, *The Waste Land*. "Its source is the *Satyricon* of Petronius, and its speaker is Trimalchio, a wealthy and vulgar freedman." Now in Fitzgerald's novel, there is a reference to Gatsby's "career as Trimalchio," and one learns from his letters that he was so impressed with this role of Gatsby's that he wanted to entitle the book *Trimalchio in West Egg*. Could Fitzgerald have been reminded of the *Satyricon* by *The Waste Land* itself?

Fitzgerald's and Eliot's pictures of society are thematically related: everywhere, at all levels of society prevail the same sterility, the same failure of love, the same empty relationships, whether it be Lil and her husband, the typist and the clerk, or Myrtle and Wilson, Tom and Daisy, Nick and Jordan, or even Gatsby and Daisy. Except for Nick, none of them can tell good from evil. Moreover, the connotations of Fitzgerald's ashes image (i.e. "dead fire") for his characters' unfaithfulness in love are the same as those of Eliot's "Fire Sermon" stigmatizing the lustful. And the oppressive heat in chapter 7 of *Gatsby* creates an unreal atmosphere. "Hot! Hot! Hot!" recalls Eliot's "Burning, burning, burning, burning." Perhaps they, too, are "burning" in hell.

One aspect of sterility is the characters' aimlessness; they do not know what to do with time. One notes a verbal correspondence between the two works; the woman in "A Game of Chess" says despairingly:

> "What shall I do now? What shall I do?
> I shall rush out as I am, and walk the street
> With my hair down, so. What shall we do to-morrow?
> What shall we ever do?"

and Daisy, first in chapter 1:

> "What'll we plan?" She turned to me helplessly: "What do people plan?"

and again in chapter 7:

> "What'll we do with ourselves this afternoon," cried Daisy, "and the day after that, and the next thirty years?"

This is a hauntingly close echo, almost word for word. "HURRY UP PLEASE IT'S TIME" echoes through *The Waste Land*, and the urgency of time is one of its leitmotifs, counterpointed with the characters' wasting of it. In *Gatsby*, clocks play a noticeable part. "The clock ticked on the washstand" as Gatsby spun his gaudy youthful dreams of the future.

At Gatsby and Daisy's first meeting after five years, in Gatsby's embarrassment, he almost breaks the clock; it thus becomes a symbol of Gatsby's wish to turn back time, to repeat the past, or to distort time. The last lines of the book pick up the theme of time again and our vain pursuit of "the orgastic future that year by year recedes before us." Fitzgerald's characters are time-wasters. Daisy sums up their inconsequential attitude this way: "Do you always watch for the longest day of the year and then miss it? I always watch for the longest day in the year and then miss it."

Life in the waste land is thus meaningless, in Eliot without spiritual meaning, and in Fitzgerald devoid of purposeful idealism. In *The Waste Land*, the wheel motif, as in the circles of Dante's hell, or the Wheel of Fortune, evokes this "death-in-life." In a novel dealing with the theme of corrupting materialism, this motif symbolizing a spiritually sterile "life in the world" would be highly appropriate. In fact, Fitzgerald's descriptions of Gatsby's parties are dominated by the notion of the aimless drifting of the crowd, like shadows (or the shades in the *Inferno*?). The wheel symbol is implicit in the image of anonymous crowds that swirl and eddy around Gatsby, the exemplar of material success. Again the wheel symbol in the notation that he has been round the world three times?

From Fitzgerald's "social criticism," one is led naturally toward the necessity for deeper analysis of the main characters. The action revolves around Daisy Fay who recalls two figures in *The Waste Land*. First, "the hyacinth girl," who appears in part 1 of *The Waste Land*:

> "You gave me hyacinths first a year ago;
> They called me the hyacinth girl."
> ... Yet when we came back late, from the Hyacinth garden,
> Your arms full, and your hair wet, I could not
> Speak and my eyes failed, I was neither
> Living nor dead, and I knew nothing,
> Looking into the heart of light, the silence.

The scene in *The Waste Land* represents the possibility of perfect, ecstatic love that fails. Here now is the scene from chapter 5 in *The Great Gatsby*, in which Daisy answers Nick's invitation to tea (to meet Gatsby, but that she is not aware of):

> Under the dripping bare lilac-trees, a large open car was coming up the drive. It stopped. Daisy's face tipped sideways beneath a three-cornered lavender hat, looked out at me with a bright ecstatic smile.
> "Is this absolutely where you live, my dearest one?"
> The exhilarating ripple of her voice was a wild tonic in the rain. I had to follow the sound of it for a moment, up and down, before any words came

through. A damp streak of hair lay like a dash of blue paint across her
cheek, and her hand was wet with glistening drops as I took it to help her
from the car.

The textual resemblances are startling: the beautiful girl with wet hair,
the presence, not of blue hyacinths, but the image of lilacs evoked through
the "bare trees," and the colors, lavender and blue, and especially the
reaction of the dumbfounded protagonist. Although Daisy seemingly offers love to Nick, as the hyacinth girl (equated in *The Waste Land* with
the Grail-bearer, which is exactly Daisy's role) did to the protagonist,
love will of course not materialize between them.

I would also point out the parallel between Daisy and Philomela,
whose story is evoked in part 2 of *The Waste Land* by a tapestry or
painting depicting:

> The change of Philomel, by the barbarous king
> So rudely forced; yet there the nightingale
> Filled all the desert with inviolable voice
> And still she cried, and still the world pursues,
> "Jug, Jug" to dirty ears.

Daisy too has been "forced" by Gatsby: "He took what he could get,
ravenously and unscrupulously ... eventually he took Daisy one still
October night, took her because he had no real right to touch her hand,"
which takes on the deeper symbolic meaning of the ravishment of the
New World ("a fresh, green breast of the New World"). It is true that
Daisy is associated with a nightingale she says she has heard "singing
away" romantically. But she herself is the nightingale. Her voice with
its "deathless song," the source of her infinite charm, ripples through
the book. But as Gatsby remarks: "Her voice is full of money." Only
" 'Jug, Jug' to dirty ears."

It is necessary now to recall the central myth of *The Waste Land*,
that of the Grail story, for a discussion of Fitzgerald's characters will be
enriched by making reference to it. Eliot's notes to *The Waste Land*
acknowledge his debt to Miss Jessie Weston's book on the Grail legend
From Ritual to Romance (1920), and to Sir James Frazer's book on an-
thropology *The Golden Bough* (1890). The Grail legend includes a number
of myths, but according to Miss Weston, the central one was that of the
Fisher King and the Waste Land. Here I quote Cleanth Brooks, who sum-
marizes this myth well:

> In the legends which she treats there, the land has been blighted by a
> curse. The crops do not grow and the animals cannot reproduce. The plight
> of the land is summed up by, and connected with, the plight of the lord

of the land, the Fisher King, who has been rendered impotent by maiming or sickness. The curse can be removed only by the appearance of a knight who will ask the meanings of the various symbols which are displayed to him in the castle. The shift in meaning from physical to spiritual sterility is easily made, and was, as a matter of fact, made in certain of the legends.

Miss Weston's thesis is that "the Grail legend was the surviving record of an initiation ritual" connected with the ancient Vegetation or Fertility rites. Eliot's poem follows her plan and much of his symbolism derives from her book, as he himself says in his notes.

Turning now to *The Great Gatsby*, one can see that the main characters of Fitzgerald's fable correspond in many ways to the key figures of the myth Eliot employed. However, *Gatsby* is not an *allegory* of *The Waste Land*, for much as in the poem where the characters "melt into" each other, their symbolical value can vary at different moments in the novel.

Before analysing the two main characters of *Gatsby*, that is, Gatsby and Nick, the narrator, one can usefully consider a minor personage, "Owl-Eyes," who is somewhat enigmatic. He appears only three times, and only in the role of a mere spectator. His presence can perhaps be more satisfactorily explained by referring to *The Waste Land*, specially to Tiresias, the soothsayer of antiquity who had figured in *Oedipus Rex*. Eliot's note informs the reader that he is "a mere spectator and not indeed 'a character' " and that he is nevertheless "the most important personage in the poem, uniting all the rest . . . What Tiresias *sees*, in fact, is the substance of the poem". Like him ("I Tiresias [. . .] perceived the scene and foretold the rest"), Owl-Eyes, a man "with enormous owl-eyed spectacles" is "blind," but perceptive. (Need we point out that the owl is the bird of wisdom, etc.) When he appears, the emphasis is put on *seeing*, through distortion and confusion, and on his "unusual quality of wonder." He alone notices that the books in Gatsby's library are real. After the first car accident in the book, he marvels, perceiving that the car has lost its wheel and gone in the ditch ("See"). But he doesn't drive, knows nothing about mechanics (part of his timelessness), and is therefore *not* a careless driver as Tom, Daisy, Jordan, and even Gatsby are all pointed out to be. Finally, of all the hundreds who used to throng around Gatsby, he is the only one to come to the funeral where, after wiping his glasses carefully, he pronounces the only compassionate words spoken about Gatsby: "The poor son-of-a-bitch."

Owl-Eyes's function in the novel seems to be to indicate to the reader what he is to believe; that there is something fine about Gatsby and something rotten about contemporary American society blind to all values but that of money. He is each time very close to the central meaning of the novel, its "truth." In this sense, he "unites" the characters, and even the Dutch sailors wondering at the New World, to their spiritual descendant, Gatsby, wondering at the green light at the end of Daisy's dock, as Tiresias does those of *The Waste Land*.

The characters sometimes blend into each other when one considers their symbolic value with regard to the *Waste Land* myth. In certain ways, Nick's role can be compared to that of Tiresias. He has a superior capacity for understanding, although he has not Tiresias' "second sight." Certainly, as a narrator, "what he sees is the substance." His stream of consciousness binds it all together. And there is one scene that is very reminiscent in tone and atmosphere of a *Waste Land* scene, in which Nick could be Tiresias. Here are the lines from "The Fire Sermon":

> At the violet hour, when the eyes and back
> Turn upward from the desk, when the human engine waits
> Like a taxi throbbing, waiting,
> I Tiresias, though blind, throbbing between two lives,
> Old man with wrinkled female breasts, can see
> At the violet hour, the evening hour that strives
> Homeward, and brings the sailor home from sea,
> The typist home at teatime,

lines that introduce the seduction of the typist by the clerk, witnessed by Tiresias. While, in *Gatsby*, Nick tells of his evenings in New York:

> I liked to walk up Fifth Avenue and pick out romantic women from the crowd and imagine that in a few minutes I was going to enter into their lives, and no one would ever know or disapprove. Sometimes, in my mind, I followed them to their apartments on the corners of hidden streets, and they turned and smiled back at me before they faded through a door into warm darkness. At the enchanted metropolitan twilight I felt a haunting loneliness sometimes, and felt it in others . . . poor young clerks who loitered in front of windows.

Coincidence not only between the "seers," but between the "seen."

Tiresias in *The Waste Land* is not only a spectator. An analogy can be drawn between Nick and Tiresias in his role as the unnamed protagonist and participant in the action of the poem, Tiresias as quester. *Gatsby* too is based upon an initiation ritual, in which Nick resembles the Grail knight who must ask the meaning of the various symbols displayed in the castle. In the American "waste land," the problem is to find out the secret of Gatsby and the "valley of ashes." Nick's role is not incidental to the novel, which unfolds as his eyes are gradually opened. He makes guesses, suppositions; he asks questions, listens, and learns.

There lies a fundamental difference between the two works, however. In the poem, the "truth" is revealed, but the waste land is not revived, because of the incapacity of the protagonist as Fisher King to receive it. In *Gatsby*, there is a moral progression implied by Nick's rejection of the East and return home to the West, which presumably is not a waste land.

It will be obvious that Gatsby in his romantic devotion to Daisy as an ideal of perfection is like the Grail knight also. Many readers have noticed that Fitzgerald uses the phrase "following a grail," and that Gatsby's watch over Daisy's house has the "sacredness of a vigil." He disparages Tom's feeling for Daisy as merely "personal," implying that his own love is on a far higher, ideal plane (a hint to the reader that this love is a symbol for the American dream). But Gatsby is *impure*; he is a bootlegger, who has tried to buy love. In fact, he plays somewhat the same role as the Fisher King in *The Waste Land*. Is it only an accident that Fitzgerald makes him a salmon fisher on Lake Superior, or that he has Tom say about Gatsby: "[Women] meet all kinds of crazy fish"? But far more significant is the fitness of this symbolism. Gatsby, instead of being maimed or impotent, is corrupt, and a materialist. Just as in the Fisher King legends, where the condition of the King entails the sterility of the land, the hero's "tragic flaw" has also created a "waste land."

Furthermore, that Fitzgerald alludes symbolically to the Fertility cults memorialized in the Grail Myths seems an inescapable conclusion. Gatsby is often connected with the sun-god. His bright yellow car "mirrored a dozen suns." He is also called a "Son of God" by Nick, a puzzling remark, out of this context. His death emphasizes this interpretation. Nick discovers Gatsby's body on a pneumatic mattress floating in the swimming pool:

> A small gust of wind that scarcely corrugated the surface was enough to disturb its accidental course with its accidental burden. The touch of a cluster of leaves revolved it slowly, tracing, like the leg of transit, a thin red circle in the water.

Why did Fitzgerald choose to have Gatsby die in this peculiar manner? Why not simply have Wilson shoot him on the steps of his mansion, for example?

One plausible answer is that the scene is a reminiscence of part 4 of *The Waste Land*, "Death by Water," relating the death of Phlebas, the Phoenician sailor, still another character the Fisher King blends into:

> Phlebas the Phoenician, a fortnight dead,
> Forgot the cry of gulls, and the deep sea swell
> And the profit and loss.

> A current under sea
> Picked his bones in whispers. As he rose and fell
> He passed the stages of his age and youth
> Entering the whirlpool.
> Gentile or Jew
> O you who turn the wheel and look to windward,
> Consider Phlebas, who was once handsome and tall as you.

On one level, Gatsby too has been a sailor, on Dan Cody's yacht, and the compass image is not only a nautical reference, but is also a link with the wheel of temporality. But on a deeper level, as Cleanth Brooks points out:

> The drowned Phoenician Sailor recalls the drowned god of the fertility cults. Miss Weston tells that each year at Alexandria an effigy of the head of the god was thrown into the water as a symbol of the death of the powers of nature, and that this head was carried by the current to Byblos where it was taken out of the water and exhibited as a symbol of the reborn god.

Foreshadowing Gatsby's death, in chapter 6, there is an odd little allusion to this ceremony when Miss Baedeker, who is drunk, complains about getting "[her] head stuck in a pool": " 'Anything I hate is to get my head stuck in a pool,' mumbled Miss Baedeker. 'They almost drowned me once over in New Jersey.' " Fitzgerald means the reader to see Gatsby as a vegetation god, or life symbol, and that is why the life-giving rain and sun accompany him. Following this interpretation, Gatsby's death would be a necessary sacrifice to regenerate the land. That explains Nick's words, when the second body, that of Wilson (by poetic justice, the murderer is the "representative" of the valley of ashes) is found: "The holocaust was complete."

One can test the hypothesis of a relationship between *The Waste Land* and *The Great Gatsby* by examining some of the seasonal and elemental symbols that structure the novel. They further support the probable relation to the primitive fertility cults having to do with the seasons, the rain and the sun, and the bringing of spring out of winter and life out of death. *Gatsby* develops within the span of time from the beginning of spring (when Nick comes to New York, "with the sunshine and great bursts of leaves on the trees") to early autumn (when he returns to the West). A single scene provides a close thematic link with *The Waste Land*, and that is Daisy and Gatsby's reunion. Indeed, Fitzgerald sets this crucial meeting in midsummer, but only early spring flowers are in bloom (jonquils, hawthorn, plum, and kiss-me-at-the-gate), as if it were a rebirth of spring, recalling the opening lines of *The Waste Land*:

> April is the cruellest month, breeding
> Lilacs out of the dead land, mixing
> Memory and desire, stirring
> Dull roots with spring rain.

How precisely Fitzgerald captures the mood of "memory and desire" in this scene! Gatsby's death occurs on the last day of summer, thus there seems to be a definite assimilation with the cycle of life.

The paradox of water in *Gatsby* is the same as in *The Waste Land* and it underlines Gatsby's ambiguity as hero and sinner. "Death by Water" is to be feared, as in the poem . . . that, with "The Fire Sermon" are echoed in Daisy's request that Nick remain watchfully in the garden: "In case there's a fire or a flood . . . or any act of God." However, Gatsby as a life-symbol is the rainmaker. "Blessed are the dead that the rain falls on," someone murmurs at Gatsby's funeral. Rain was significantly associated with Daisy, too, when she and Gatsby met again, and always in the liquid notes of her famous voice that recall the "water-dripping" song of the hermit thrush in Eliot's poem and notes. The recurrence of this rain symbol in *Gatsby*, then, seems to be a device to suggest that idealism and imagination are life-giving. Nick's final judgment, with its water/ dust imagery, stresses this:

> No . . . Gatsby turned out all right at the end; it is what preyed on Gatsby, what foul dust floated in the wake of his dreams that temporarily closed out my interest in the abortive sorrows and short-winded elations of men.

The thunder at the conclusion of *The Waste Land* rumbles: "Datta," "Dayadhovam," "Damyatta," which Eliot explains in the notes signify: "Give," "Sympathize," "Control," words that contain the moral "lesson" of the poem. The moral theme of *Gatsby* is the same; it is conveyed pointedly, both positively and negatively. The commandments are obeyed or disobeyed through the acts of the main characters. The denizens of the waste land *take*, but do not *give*. Gatsby also succumbed to this rapaciousness, but he is "saved" by the generosity of his idealism. Nick refuses to profit by Gatsby's clumsy offer of a "connection" in payment for his friendship. *Sympathize:* Gatsby is deserted by all in the end, except for Owl-Eyes, and Nick, who has always lent a sympathetic ear to his neighbor. *Control:* one of Fitzgerald's major themes in *Gatsby* is the carelessness of the people in the waste land, symbolized by their careless driving:

> They were careless people, Tom and Daisy . . . they smashed up things and then retreated back into their money or their vast carelessness, or

whatever it was that kept them together, and let other people clean up the mess they made. . . .

Ironically, it is Daisy who asks Tom in the midst of a row to: "Please have a little self-control," to which he responds indignantly. Gatsby has been stopped for speeding, but he is always portrayed as poised, never drunk, in the midst of wild parties . . . Finally, Nick, who is the moral exemplar and "one of the few honest people that [he has] ever known," goes home wanting the world to stand "at a sort of moral attention forever." One can now hazard a guess as to why Gatsby did not materialize for Fitzgerald. As he wrote to Max Perkins (circa Dec. 20, 1924): "I myself didn't know what Gatsby looked like or was engaged in." Some of his readers criticized Fitzgerald for this "vagueness," too. In fact, his hero's symbolic charge was perhaps too great. Gatsby was an idea, not a character.

The argument of this paper has been that *The Waste Land* was a seminal work for F. Scott Fitzgerald when he wrote *The Great Gatsby*. It must be admitted that the general similarity in themes could be simply the "ideas in the air," the disenchantment and world-weariness of the post World War I era expressed by many writers such as Spengler. But it is the coherent, intricate network of significant details and what can only be specific allusions that points to a kind of *permeation* of *Gatsby* by *The Waste Land*. Also, the fact that analysis in this perspective is illuminating and makes apparently irrelevant details come clear and fit into a rich, carefully wrought pattern or musical structure indicates that in Eliot's myths and symbols Fitzgerald found an "objective correlative" for his uniquely American tale.

Chronology

1896	F. Scott Fitzgerald born September 24, in St. Paul, Minnesota.
1911–13	Attends Newman Academy in Hackensack, New Jersey.
1913–17	Attends Princeton University, but leaves before graduation to enter the army. Sees no overseas service.
1919	Discharged from the army in February.
1920	Publishes *This Side of Paradise.* Marries Zelda Sayre.
1921	Publishes *Flappers and Philosophers.*
1922	Publishes *The Beautiful and Damned* and *Tales of the Jazz Age.* Daughter Frances born in St. Paul. Family moves to Great Neck, Long Island.
1923	Play, *The Vegetable,* fails in Atlantic City.
1924	Family moves to the Riviera.
1925	Publishes *The Great Gatsby.*
1926	Publishes *All the Sad Young Men.*
1927	Begins to write scripts in Hollywood; family moves to house near Wilmington, Delaware.
1930	Zelda has nervous breakdown in Paris.
1931	Returns to Hollywood as scriptwriter.
1932	Family moves to a house near Rodgers Forge, Maryland.
1934	Publishes *Tender Is the Night.*
1935	Publishes *Taps at Reveille.* Period of "crack-up" begins.
1937	Moves back to Hollywood as scriptwriter. Relationship with Sheilah Graham.
1940	Dies in Hollywood on December 21. He is buried in Rockville, Maryland.
1948	Zelda Fitzgerald dies in a fire at a sanitarium.

Contributors

Harold Bloom, Sterling Professor of the Humanities at Yale University, is the author of *The Anxiety of Influence, Poetry and Repression,* and many other volumes of literary criticism. His forthcoming study, *Freud: Transference and Authority,* attempts a full-scale reading of all of Freud's major writings. A MacArthur Prize Fellow, he is the general editor of The Chelsea House Library of Literary Criticism.

Kenneth Eble is Professor of English at the University of Utah. His books include studies of American higher education, and of Howells and of Fitzgerald.

Marius Bewley was Professor of English at Rutgers University. His books include *The Complex Fate* and *The Eccentric Design.*

David Parker teaches English at the University of Malaya, and has published articles on Shakespeare and on Chaucer.

Ron Neuhaus teaches English at The University of Wisconsin, River Falls.

Keath Fraser teaches English at the University of Calgary. He has published articles in American, British, and Canadian journals.

A. B. Paulson is Assistant Professor of English at Hamilton College.

Brian Way is the author of *Audience Participation, Development through Drama,* and *F. Scott Fitzgerald and the Art of Social Fiction.*

Letha Audhuy is a Professor at the Université de Toulouse-le-Mirail.

Bibliography

Barrett, William. "Fitzgerald and America." *Partisan Review*, 18 (May–June 1951), 345–53.

Bishop, John Peale. "The Missing All." *Virginia Quarterly Review*, 12 (Winter 1937), 107–21.

Bruccoli, Matthew J. *Some Sort of Epic Grandeur: The Life of F. Scott Fitzgerald.* New York: Harcourt Brace Jovanovich, 1981.

Callaghan, Morley. *That Summer in Paris: Memories of Tangled Friendships with Hemingway, Fitzgerald, and Some Others.* New York: Coward-McCann, 1963.

Callahan, John F. *The Illusions of a Nation: Myth and History in the Novels of F. Scott Fitzgerald.* Urbana: University of Illinois Press, 1972.

Cowley, Malcolm. "Fitzgerald: The Double Man." *Saturday Review*, 34 (February 24, 1951), 9–10, 42–44.

Cowley, Malcolm and Robert Cowley. *Fitzgerald and the Jazz Age.* New York: Charles Scribner's Sons, 1966.

Eble, Kenneth Eugene. *F. Scott Fitzgerald.* Rev. ed. Boston: Twayne Publishers, 1977.

———, ed. *F. Scott Fitzgerald: A Collection of Criticism.* New York: McGraw-Hill, 1973.

Fahey, William A. *F. Scott Fitzgerald and the American Dream.* New York: Thomas Y. Crowell Co., Publishers, 1973.

The Fitzgerald-Hemingway Annual. Edited by Matthew J. Bruccoli. Washington, D.C.: NCR Microcard Editions, 1969–.

Flahiff, F. T. "*The Great Gatsby:* Scott Fitzgerald's Chaucerian Rag." In *Figures in a Ground: Canadian Essays on Modern Literature in Honor of Sheila Watson,* edited by Diane Bessai and David Jackel. Saskatoon, Saskatchewan: Western Producer Prairie Books, 1978, 87–97.

Friedrich, Otto. "F. Scott Fitzgerald: Money, Money, Money." *American Scholar*, 29 (Summer 1960), 392–405.

Geismar, Maxwell. "F. Scott Fitzgerald: Orestes at the Ritz." In *The Last of the Provincials: The American Novel 1915–1925.* Boston: Houghton Mifflin, 1943.

Greenfield, Howard. *F. Scott Fitzgerald.* New York: Crown Publishers, 1974.

Hindus, Milton. *F. Scott Fitzgerald: An Introduction and Interpretation.* New York: Holt, Rinehart and Winston, 1968.

Kazin, Alfred. *F. Scott Fitzgerald: The Man and His Work.* Cleveland: World Publishing Co., 1951.

Laird, David. "Hallucination and History in *The Great Gatsby.*" *South Dakota Review*, 15, no. 1 (1977), 18–27.

Lehan, Richard Daniel. *F. Scott Fitzgerald and the Craft of Fiction.* Carbondale: Southern Illinois University Press, 1966.

Lockridge, Ernest, ed. *Twentieth-Century Interpretations of "The Great Gatsby": A Collection of Critical Essays.* Englewood Cliffs, N.J.: Prentice-Hall, Inc., 1968.

Miller, James E., Jr. *F. Scott Fitzgerald: His Art and Technique.* New York: New York University Press, 1964.

Mizener, Arthur. *The Far Side of Paradise: A Biography of F. Scott Fitzgerald.* Boston: Houghton Mifflin, 1951.

————, ed. *F. Scott Fitzgerald: A Collection of Critical Essays.* Englewood Cliffs, N.J.: Prentice-Hall, Inc., 1963.

Modern Fiction Studies 7, no. 1 (1961). Special Fitzgerald Issue.

Monroe, H. Keith. "Gatsby and the Gods." *Renascence,* 31, no. 1 (1978), 51–63.

Stallman, Robert W. "Conrad and *The Great Gatsby.*" *Twentieth-Century Literature,* I (April 1955), 5–12.

Stern, Milton R. *The Golden Moment: The Novels of F. Scott Fitzgerald.* Urbana: University of Illinois Press, 1970.

Trower, Katherine B. "Visions of Paradise in *The Great Gatsby.*" *Renascence,* 25, no. 1 (1972), 14–23.

Turnbull, Andrew. *Scott Fitzgerald.* New York: Charles Scribner's Sons, 1962.

Way, Brian. *F. Scott Fitzgerald and the Art of Social Fiction.* London: Edward Arnold, 1980.

West, Rebecca. *Ending in Earnest.* Garden City, N.Y.: Doubleday, 1931.

Acknowledgments

"The Structure of *The Great Gatsby*" by Kenneth Eble from *F. Scott Fitzgerald* by Kenneth Eble, copyright © 1977 by G. K. Hall & Co. Reprinted by permission.

"Scott Fitzgerald's Criticism of America" by Marius Bewley from *The Sewanee Review*, copyright © 1954 by The University of the South. Reprinted by permission.

"Two Versions of the Hero" by David Parker from *English Studies*, copyright © 1973 by Swets & Zeitlinger B.V., Amsterdam. Reprinted by permission.

"Gatsby and the Failure of the Omniscient 'I' " by Ron Neuhaus from *The Denver Quarterly*, copyright © 1977 by The University of Denver. Reprinted by permission.

"Another Reading of *The Great Gatsby*" by Keath Fraser from *English Studies in Canada*, copyright © 1979 by the Association of Canadian University Teachers of English. Reprinted by permission.

"Oral Aggression and Splitting" by A. B. Paulson from *American Imago*, copyright © 1979 by the Association for Applied Psychoanalysis, Inc. Reprinted by permission.

"The Great Gatsby" by Brian Way from *F. Scott Fitzgerald and the Art of Social Fiction* by Brian Way, copyright © 1980 by Brian Way. Reprinted by permission of Edward Arnold Ltd.

"*The Waste Land* Myth and Symbols in *The Great Gatsby*" by Letha Audhuy from *Etudes Anglaises*, copyright © 1980 by Didier-Erudition, Paris. Reprinted by permission.

Index

A

"Absolution," 6, 76
Alger, Horatio, 89
ambiguity, 58
ambivalence, 55, 84
American Dream, 11–27, 62, 85, 111
    anti-Calvinistic, 11
    Gatsby and, 11–27
American romantic hero, 14
Anderson, Quentin, 73
Arthurian romances, 39
Austen, Jane, 43
"Awkward Age, The," 87
    Great Gatsby and, 87

B

Barzun, Jacques, 14
Belasco, David, 41
"Belle Dame Sans Merci, La," 1, 3
Boy Who Killed His Mother, The, 78, 82
Brooks, Cleanth, 116
Browning, Robert, 30, 43
Buchanan, Daisy,
    Belle Dame Sans Merci and, 3
    green light and, 19–21
    levels, 18–19
    Myrtle and, 79–81

C

Calvin, John, 47
Calvinism, 11
Carrithers, Gale, Jr., 73
Childe Roland to the Dark Tower Came, 30–35, 39, 41
Citizen Kane, 105
Civil War, 107
Col. David Crockett's Exploits, 14
comedy, 101–4
Conrad, Joseph, 46, 109
Cowley, Malcolm, 77
"Crack-up, The," 77
criticism, 71
Crockett, Davy, 17, 100
Cronin, A. J., 21

D

Dante, 115
David Copperfield, 39
Dickens, Charles, 101–2

E

Eliot, T. S., 17, 46, 94, 109–22
English literature, 29
Erikson, Erik, 73, 75
Esquire, 77
Eve of St. Agnes, The, 2

F

Fall of Hyperion, The, 1
Falstaff, 102–3, 106
Faulkner, William, 46
Fiedler, Leslie, 61, 65
"Fire Sermon," 114, 118
Fitzgerald, F. Scott, 1, 8, 23
    ambivalence, 75
    biography, 65, 66, 77
    comic vision, 102
    Eliot and, 109–22
    feminine characters, 61
    greatest novels, 1, 96
    letters, 45, 61, 74
    personal life, 1
    sexual ambiguity, 65
    short stories, 59
    Spenser and, 3
    style, 8, 9
    technique, 75
Fitzgerald, Zelda, 1
Flaubert, Gustave, 97
Ford, Ford Maddox, 46
Franklin, Benjamin, 89
Frazer, James (Sir), 116
Freud, Sigmund, 71, 75, 77, 79–81
From Ritual to Romance, 116
Full Moon in March, A, 3

G

"Game of Chess, A," 111, 113, 114
Gatsby, Jay, 14, 17, 27
    American Dream and, 27, 29
    death, 26, 27, 100, 103, 119–21
    mythic character, 17–19
    mythic quality, 20
    naivete, 21
    Platonic conception of himself, 7, 15, 62, 75, 104
    romantic hero, 17, 38, 40
    romanticism, 27, 98
    symbolic role, 22
    Tom Buchanan and, 24
    vision, 16
"Gerontion," 94, 111
Golden Bough, The, 116
Good Soldier, The, 46
Grail legend, 117–19
Grail myths, 119
Grapes of Wrath, The, 92
Great Gatsby, The
    American Dream, 11–27
    Anglo-Saxon, 29
    autobiographical, 76, 77
    bad writing, 98

Bruccoli edition, 58
center, 6, 7
Childe Roland, 30–35
construction, 89
criticism, 11, 109
doubling, 75
end, 71, 84, 88, 99, 100, 107
English literature, 29
facsimile of manuscript, 58, 59
galley proofs, 7, 9
Gerontion, 94
green light, 3, 19–21, 24, 97, 118
hero, 14, 29–44
introduction, 5
Jazz Age, 11
Madame Bovary, 96
manuscript, 67
momentum, 6
mood, 6
moral theme, 110
myth, 14
narrative technique, 45–55
order, 7
organization, 73
plot, 5–7
resolution, 7
revisions, 8–9
rhetoric, 50, 53, 54
romantic vision, 13
structure, 5–9, 49
    flaws, 51
theme, 11, 68, 73, 76
"valley of ashes," 49
view of wealth, 13
waste land, 32–34
Wasteland, 109–122
Great Good Place, The, 16

H
Heart of Darkness, 46, 54
Hemingway, Ernest, 1
Henry IV, 104, 106
hero, 16, 29–32, 35, 43
    tragic, 103
    romantic, 31, 35, 40, 41, 43
Holland, Norman, 78

I
illusion, 73, 93, 104
imagery, 72, 82, 83
Inferno, 115
irony, 47, 49, 51, 90, 97

J
James, Henry, 16, 30, 87
    later fiction, 87

Jazz Age, 11, 14, 20, 23, 94, 111
Jefferson, Thomas, 12
Joyce, James, 46

K
Keats, John, 1–3
    Fitzgerald and, 2
Klein, Melanie, 75
Kohut, 75
Kubla Khan, 105

L
Lamia, 1
Lampl De Groot, Jeanne, 80
Last Judgment, 33
Last Tycoon, The, 9
Lec, Stanislaw, 1
Lockridge, Ernest, H., 74
Lord Jim, 54
"Love in the Night," 94

M
Madame Bovary, 96
Mailer, Norman, 1
manuscript, 67
Mencken, H. L., 100
metaphor, 49, 52, 66, 72, 73
Mizener, Arthur, 65, 77
modern novel, 97
morality, 42, 83, 101, 107
Morte d'Arthur, 39
myth, 1, 14, 17, 18, 100, 116, 119
    mythic characters, 17, 18
"Myths for Materialists," 14

N
narrator, 6, 7, 35, 37, 40, 45–55, 63, 66–69, 79, 82, 108, 111, 117
Nero, 105
Nineteenth-century fiction, 97
Nostromo, 96
notebooks, 66

O
Oedipus Rex, 117

P
"Paleface and Redskin," 30
Perkins, Maxwell, 61, 66, 74, 96, 109, 122
Petronius, 68, 105, 114
Piper, Henry D., 76
Plato, 57, 68
Plaza Hotel, 88
Princeton University, 65
Puritan tradition, 11

R
Rahv, Philip, 30, 43
reality, 42, 52
    illusion and, 42, 49, 62, 93
"Rich Boy, The," 59, 66, 68, 70
Romantic dream, 73
Romantic sensibility, 108
Romanticism, 27, 43, 73, 93, 97
Round Table, 39

S
Sangreal, 29
Satyricon, The, 58, 60, 69, 105, 114
    Great Gatsby and, 60, 69
Scribner's, 74, 109
sexuality, 65, 68–71, 78, 79, 81–84
Shelley, Percy Bysshe, 3
Smith, Grahame, 101–2
Spengler, Oswald, 122
Spenser, Edmund, 3
Stallman, R. W., 75
Stendhal, 97
Stern, Milton, 73
symbols, 22, 24, 25, 33, 82, 91, 100, 109, 116
Symposium, The, 57

T
Tacitus, 105

Tender Is the Night, 61, 65
This Side of Paradise, 92
time, 39–40, 114–115
Tiresias, 117, 118
Triangle Club, 65, 66
Trilling, Lionel, 1, 82
Trimalchio, 100, 105, 106, 114
Trimalchio in West Egg, 105, 114

V
Vanity Fair, 96
Victorian sensibility, 33

W
Waste Land, The, 23, 109–22
wealth, 13
Welles, Orson, 105
Weston, Jessie, 116, 117
Wharton, Edith, 100, 102
Whitman, Walt, 30
Wilson, Edmund, 45
Woolf, Virginia, 61
"World Fair," 82
World Series, 34
World War I, 45
World's Fair, 61, 104
Wuthering Heights, 35

Y
Yeats, William Butler, 3